# Praise for *Tell Me the Stories of Jesus*

"As is true of all of Dr. Mohler's work, *Tell Me the Stories of Jesus* is thorough, thought-provoking, and easy to understand. Jesus' parables are masterfully intertwined with church history, profound theological truth, and practical application so that the reader not only understands Scripture better, but has a deeper desire to follow Christ. Whether you're a new believer or a lifelong Christian, this book will draw your heart toward the things of God."

—Allie Beth Stuckey, commentator and host of the podcast Relatable

"If you are preaching through the parables, teaching through them in a series, or simply reading for edification and devotion, *Tell Me the Stories of Jesus* will be a welcome companion. Having benefited from reading this book myself, I eagerly commend it to you, and plan to return to it as I preach and teach on the matchless stories of our Savior contained in these precious passages."

—Ligon Duncan, chancellor, Reformed Theological Seminary

"The parables are some of the most familiar parts of Jesus' teaching—so simple that a child can grasp them, yet so mysterious that a lifetime of reflection is hardly enough time to plumb their collective depths. In this book, Dr. Mohler offers the reader an account that does justice to both aspects, pointing us to the simple message of the kingdom they convey and to the complex problems of the human heart they reveal. There are many books about the parables, but this one has the pleasing strength of combining clarity and learning with pastoral care and gospel urgency. A fine volume from an accomplished Bible teacher."

— Carl R. Trueman, Professor of Biblical and
Religious Studies, Grove City College.

"Dr. Mohler's treatment of the parables of Jesus succeeds magnificently at showing their explosive power. In his hands, the parables are never ho-hum tales designed to coddle the saints, but world-transforming stories designed to burst with the power of the kingdom of God."

— D. A. Carson, a Distinguished Emeritus Professor of New
Testament at Trinity Evangelical Divinity School and
president and cofounder of the Gospel Coalition

"In this crisp and clear exposition of the parables of Jesus, Al Mohler brings together the ancient world with contemporary life, unpacking the original meaning of the parables and then applying them to current circumstances and situations. Mohler also skillfully interprets the parables in light of the storyline of the Gospels and indeed the entire Bible, treating us to a profound theological reflection on the meaning of the parables. Preachers, teachers, and laypersons will find much help in this accessible treatment of Jesus' most famous stories."

— Tom Schreiner, the James Buchanan Harrison Professor of New Testament Interpretation, Southern Baptist Theological Seminary

"Al Mohler's edifying, enlightening study of Jesus' parables is broad, but concise. It is rich, but digestible. It is presented by a first-rate theologian, but is written in a manner that will minister to the newest of Christians."

— Mike Fabarez, founding pastor, Compass Bible Church, South Orange County, California

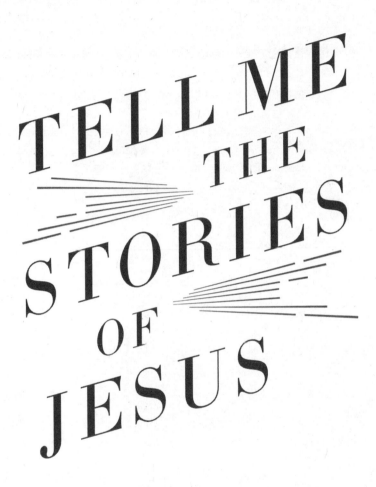

TELL ME THE STORIES OF JESUS

THE EXPLOSIVE POWER
OF JESUS' PARABLES

# TELL ME
# THE
# STORIES
# OF
# JESUS

R. ALBERT MOHLER JR.

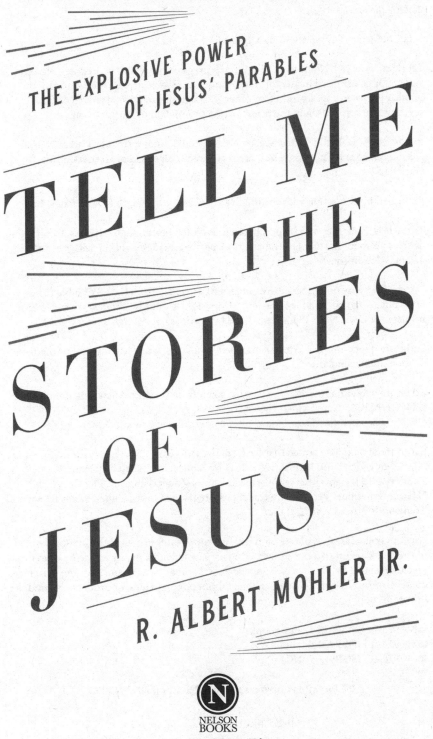

NELSON
BOOKS

An Imprint of Thomas Nelson

*Tell Me the Stories of Jesus*

Published in Nashville, Tennessee, by Nelson Books, an imprint of Thomas Nelson. Nelson Books and Thomas Nelson are registered trademarks of HarperCollins Christian Publishing, Inc.

Published in association with the literary agency of Wolgemuth & Associates, Inc.

Thomas Nelson titles may be purchased in bulk for educational, business, fundraising, or sales promotional use. For information, please e-mail SpecialMarkets@ ThomasNelson.com.

Unless otherwise noted, Scripture quotations are taken from the ESV® Bible (The Holy Bible, English Standard Version®). Copyright © 2001 by Crossway, a publishing ministry of Good News Publishers. Used by permission. All rights reserved.

Scripture quotations marked DRA are taken from the Douay-Rheims 1899 American Edition. Public domain.

Scripture quotations marked NASB95 are taken from the New American Standard Bible® (NASB95). Copyright © 1960, 1962, 1963, 1968, 1971, 1972, 1973, 1975, 1977, 1995 by The Lockman Foundation. Used by permission. www.lockman.org

Scripture quotations marked NIV are from the Holy Bible, New International Version®, NIV®. Copyright © 1973, 1978, 1984, 2011 by Biblica, Inc.® Used by permission of Zondervan. All rights reserved worldwide. www.Zondervan.com. The "NIV" and "New International Version" are trademarks registered in the United States Patent and Trademark Office by Biblica, Inc.®

Any internet addresses, phone numbers, or company or product information printed in this book are offered as a resource and are not intended in any way to be or to imply an endorsement by Thomas Nelson, nor does Thomas Nelson vouch for the existence, content, or services of these sites, phone numbers, companies, or products beyond the life of this book.

ISBN 978-0-7180-9925-1 (audiobook)
ISBN 978-0-7180-9922-0 (eBook)
ISBN 978-0-7180-9916-9 (HC)

**Library of Congress Control Number: 2022932998**

*Printed in the United States of America*

22  23  24  25  26   LSC   10  9  8  7  6  5  4  3  2  1

Dedicated to
Mary Margaret Barnes

*Let the children come to me, and do not hinder them,*
*for to such belongs the kingdom of God.*
Luke 18:16

*Like your mother before you, you have grabbed our hearts*
*and never let go. You are an unspeakably wonderful grand-*
*daughter, a precious gift from God and a sign of the Father's*
*promise. You are beautiful and sweet, brightening our hearts*
*and lifting our spirits. You are an infant, beautiful and*
*bright, and sheer delight. Your faithful parents love you with*
*unbreakable and joyous love. Your two big brothers adore*
*you. Grammie and I love you more than you can imagine.*
*Just to think of you is to smile and to thank God for such a*
*gift. I pray for the day when you will come to know the Lord*
*Jesus Christ as your Savior and confess the faith once deliv-*
*ered to the saints. Who knows? God may draw you to himself*
*through one of the parables of Jesus.*

*The only thing to surpass loving you as granddaughter*
*would be loving you as sister in Christ.*
Papa

# Contents

Introduction                                                                    xi

Chapter 1:    Why Do You Speak to Them in Parables?              1
Chapter 2:    Hearts Ready to Receive the Word                      11
Chapter 3:    The Children of Light and the Children
              of Darkness                                           25
Chapter 4:    And Who Is My Neighbor?                               35
Chapter 5:    Even If One Should Rise from the Dead                 47
Chapter 6:    Redemption, Rejoicing, and Rejection in
              Luke 15                                               61
Chapter 7:    What Will He Do to Those Tenants?                     79
Chapter 8:    Unworthy Guests                                       95
Chapter 9:    When the Son of Man Comes, Will He
              Find Faith on Earth?                                  105
Chapter 10:   The Exalted Humbled and the Humble
              Exalted                                               115
Chapter 11:   The Shrewd Sons of This Age                           131
Chapter 12:   Miserly Fairness Versus Extravagant Grace            141
Chapter 13:   Well Done, Good and Faithful Servant                 151
Chapter 14:   So Also My Heavenly Father Will Do to You            161
Chapter 15:   The Kingdom of Heaven Is Like This                    173
Chapter 16:   When the Son of Man Comes in His Glory               193
Chapter 17:   You Know Neither the Day Nor the Hour                203

# CONTENTS

*Acknowledgments*                                      215

*Notes*                                                219

*About the Author*                                     221

# Introduction

Jesus came into Galilee, proclaiming the gospel of God,
and saying, "The time is fulfilled, and the kingdom of
God is at hand; repent and believe in the gospel."

—MARK 1:14-15

Jesus came preaching the gospel of God—and he came telling stories. The most famous of Jesus' stories are the parables. They are not tame stories intended to deliver sentimental messages. They are not moralistic, like Aesop's famed fables. They are not fairy tales, such as the kind that abounded in medieval Europe. Nor are they stories intended for children, though children are often among the first to understand them. In the parables, Jesus was not concerned with mere self-improvement or trite moral messages. Not at all.

God's own Son, God in human flesh, is who shared the parables with us. For this reason, Jesus' parables reveal nothing less than the kingdom of heaven and the power of almighty God expressed in both judgment and grace. They illuminate God's character and the hardness of sinful human hearts.

Sometimes the parables drew sinners into the kingdom of God. Sometimes they confused the very people who heard Jesus tell them. Their confusion often revealed a spiritual blindness and hardness of heart.

The parables are like hand grenades. Jesus took them out and set them before his hearers. Then . . . he pulled the pin out. Listen carefully, because the parable explodes. If you miss the blast of the story, you have missed the power of the parable. There is a reason that Jesus' parables are so memorable. We simply can't shake them. We can't escape them. We can't forget them.

All too often, the parables angered Jesus' listeners because they recognized that he was speaking not just *to* them but *about* them.

We may think that the power of the parables comes through our achievement in understanding them, but Jesus told his disciples that they only understood the parables because God's grace had opened their eyes to see and their ears to hear. The same is true for us. In actuality, it may not be so much that we understand the parables as that the parables understand *us*.

One who hears Jesus' parables—really hears them—is counted in the kingdom of heaven. Those who refuse to hear the parables are in the kingdom of Satan, the Evil One. Jesus told us this himself.

The parables opened hearts to receive eternal life and the forgiveness of sins, but the parables also made some people so angry that they were determined to kill Jesus. And kill him they did.

## Why Are We So Drawn to Stories?

To be human is to be drawn to stories—powerfully drawn. Just watch a middle school child as she walks into a room and sees a parent reading a storybook to her little brother. She knows the story. It was read to her over and over again when she was younger. She can recite it almost verbatim. But she cannot resist sitting down and hearing the story once more. She already knows where to smile, where to laugh, and where to cry. She listens anyway, and she listens intently. She smiles and laughs and cries all over again. She can't help it. She finds joy in her little brother's smiling in all the right places. The only thing better than hearing a story is sharing the story.

Our earliest memories are linked to the stories we were told and the truths those stories revealed to us. We learn some of the central truths of our lives by means of stories. In fact, our lives are lived out in the framework of a story. Just try saying anything important about yourself without some kind of story: where you were born, where you went to school, the events that help your life make sense. Human beings are not merely *homo sapiens*, the thinking beings. We are also *homo narratus*, the storytelling beings.

The gospel of Jesus Christ is itself a story. Even the most succinct summary of the gospel is narrative in form: "For God so loved the world, that he gave his only Son, that whoever believes in him should not perish but have eternal life" (John 3:16). The verse is short, but it contains a supremely powerful message in the form of narrative. In just a few words, Jesus tells us about the love of God, the fact that Jesus is the Son of God, the reason why he came to take on human flesh, the centrality of belief in Jesus, and the power of the gospel to promise eternal life.

The most influential confession of faith in the history of the church, the Apostles' Creed, also takes the form of a story. It begins: "I believe in God, the Father Almighty, Maker of heaven and earth, and in Jesus Christ, his only Son, our Lord, who was conceived of the Holy Ghost, born of the Virgin Mary, suffered under Pontius Pilate, was crucified, dead, and buried. He descended into hell. The third day he rose again from the dead. He ascended into heaven and sits at the right hand of God the Father Almighty, whence he shall come to judge the quick and the dead."

Stories are vital for how we understand the Bible. The Bible itself, taken as a whole, unfolds the unified story of God's redeeming love and infinite glory. Both the Old and New Testaments include vast sections of historical material that, as Francis Schaeffer used to say, should be taken in the normal sense of space, time, and history. The Bible is inspired by the Holy Spirit—every word of it—and the history it contains is absolutely true in the historical sense: real people, real places, real events.

Genesis begins with the narrative of God's creation of the world and of all the creatures within it, including the one creature made in his own image—human beings. The Old Testament goes on to tell the history of God's love for Israel and the events that set the stage for the revelation of the gospel of Jesus Christ. The New Testament Gospels (Matthew, Mark, Luke, and John) reveal Jesus' life and ministry. The book of Acts tells the history of the early church.

Within the big story of redemption and the historical narratives found throughout the Bible, we also encounter stories told by various people—including Jesus' parables. As we will see, Jesus was not the first teacher to use parables. But he spoke parables in a different way—with infinitely greater authority than any other teacher. As one of my seminary professors put it, "Jesus did not invent parables; he merely perfected the art."[1] The truth of that assessment is revealed by the fact that today, more than two thousand years later, even people who have little connection to Christianity talk about prodigal children and the good Samaritan.

## What Is a Parable, Anyway?

At the most basic level, a parable is a comparison story, using simile or metaphor to help listeners move from a familiar reality to a deeper understanding of an important truth. Sometimes, the comparison is obvious, as when Jesus begins a parable with words such as, "The kingdom of heaven is like a mustard seed." Parables that begin with a simple comparison usually open a window for our understanding, revealing and clarifying truths about the kingdom of God. At other times, the comparison is much more elaborate and embedded within the narrative, as when Jesus tells the parable of the sower. When Jesus begins a parable with characters taking action (for example, "A sower went out to sow"), watch out—an explosive comparison is coming, and the story will vastly expand your understanding of how the gospel works in human hearts.

Sometimes, we learn best through a story that makes us see what we would otherwise miss. Stories can drive a truth deep into the human heart when nothing else can. The parables are powerful precisely because they catch us off guard.

I define the parables of Jesus as *surprising stories and word pictures drawn from the familiar, that powerfully reveal to us the unfamiliar.* Jesus starts with what we can easily see in order to help us see what only he can show us—the realities of the kingdom of heaven. We can see a farmer sowing seed. The original hearers of the parable of the sower might have been watching such a farmer as Jesus was speaking. But even if we do not see the sowing farmer with our eyes, we can see him in our imaginations. Jesus takes us from the farmer sowing seed to an understanding of the gospel, how it is spread and how it is received. The explosion comes, as is usually the case, at the end of the parable— the revelation of the infinite power of the gospel to transform lives and bring a harvest. Jesus takes us from what we *do* see to what we *don't* see—until he shows us in the parable.

One commentator described Jesus' parables as "designed to make one stabbing truth flash out at a man the moment he heard it."[2] That is precisely right. There is nowhere to hide when Jesus' parables come at us with their stabbing truth.

As a young Christian, I often heard a parable described as "an earthly story with a heavenly meaning." That's not a bad description, but the parables are not just about heaven; they are about the *kingdom of heaven*, the kingdom of God. They are about faithfulness in the present as much as they are about God's promises for the future. They are about God's reign, now and in the kingdom in its future fullness. They are about the good news—the gospel—and none of them is to be understood apart from the gospel.

John MacArthur got it right when he described the parables of Jesus as "ingeniously simple word pictures with profound spiritual lessons."[3] There is not one unnecessary word in any of the parables—and we need every single word Jesus gave us. A parable can be one sentence, or it may be several paragraphs. Usually, Jesus told parables that were short narrative packages. Sometimes, he told several parables in one teaching, such as the parables of lostness and foundness in Luke 15. Sometimes, Jesus told the same parable more than once, with slightly varied versions appearing in the gospels of Matthew, Mark, and Luke. This should not surprise us, since Jesus taught in so many different contexts to so many different people.

And yet, the main audience for the parables was always the disciples. Jesus not only told the parables in the hearing of the disciples, he often told parables addressed *only* to them. When he explained a parable, he explained it only to his close followers. In other words, Jesus intended his parables mainly for the church, for believing Christians. For believers, the parables are a great gift. They are *our* stories, but we want them to be overheard by the world.

We refer to Matthew, Mark, and Luke as the Synoptic Gospels because they follow a similar structure and sequence. "Synoptic" comes from a Greek word that means "to see together." The church has always recognized the similarities in content, as well as the difference in strategies, of the first three gospels. It is significant that all three of these gospels contain parables. As a matter of fact, parables take up more than one-third (35 percent) of the entire content of Matthew, Mark, and Luke. The Gospel of John contains no parables of similar structure. John's gospel follows a different line in telling us the story of Jesus. He began with the role of the preexistent Son of God in creation, the eternal Word through whom the world was made, and then the incarnation of the Son of God in human flesh (John 1:14). We need all four gospels, with each revealing to us important dimensions of Jesus' story. If the Gospels covered the same content in basically similar ways, we would not need more than one. But in his kindness, God has given us four authoritative gospels, each with its own emphases, so that we could have a full understanding of the life and ministry of Jesus—and a full collection of the parables.

Among the three Synoptic Gospels, some of the parables are unique to just one gospel, while others appear in two or all three gospels. Matthew and Luke contain the greatest number of parables, and both gospels give us insights into the context of the parables. Mark, the shortest of the four gospels, contains the fewest that are unique to one gospel.

## Does the Old Testament Include Parables?

The Old Testament contains some stories similar to the parables of Jesus in the New Testament, but they are not as common as you might think. Old Testament parables most often came from prophets who were making a point. The prophets Ezekiel and Amos used parables, and in some sense the entire book of the prophet Hosea is an extended parable about Israel's spiritual infidelity. In Ecclesiastes 9:13–16, we find a parable about a poor wise man and God's vindication of wisdom.

Perhaps the most famous Old Testament parable was the one the prophet Nathan told King David. The king had committed heinous sin and had arranged a death in order to cover his sin. God knew of his grotesque sin, and so did God's prophet Nathan. Confronting the king (never a safe course of action), Nathan chose to tell the king a parable, recorded in 2 Samuel 12:1–6. Nathan told of two men, one rich and one poor. The rich man had a vast herd of sheep, but the poor man had only one sheep, which he cared for and loved. The rich man had a guest, but rather than feed the guest one of his own sheep, he stole the poor man's sheep and served it instead. David was incensed by the rich man's crime and told the prophet, "As the LORD lives, the man who has done this deserves to die." With unswerving courage, Nathan the prophet famously said to the king, "You are the man!" (v. 7). The king's conscience was awakened and he was convicted of his sin by the prophet's use of the parable.

We encounter another Old Testament parable in Isaiah's description of Israel as God's vineyard in Isaiah 5:1–7. God had made his covenant with Israel, pouring out care and protection. But Israel had repaid God's kindness with outright rebellion and idolatry. Isaiah likened Israel's sin to a carefully tended vineyard yielding to its devoted owner nothing more than bitter wild grapes. Isaiah revealed God's love song concerning his vineyard—Israel—and he documented God's charges against the people God so loved.

The Hebrew word that is translated as "parable" is *mashal*, and it is sometimes broadened to include proverbs and similar statements. Most importantly, Matthew explained Jesus' use of parables as the fulfillment of a promise (Matt. 13:35). As we read in Psalm 78:1–4,

Give ear, O my people, to my teaching;
 incline your ears to the words of my mouth!
I will open my mouth in a parable;
 I will utter dark sayings from of old,
things that we have heard and known,
 that our fathers have told us.
We will not hide them from their children,
 but tell to the coming generation
the glorious deeds of the LORD, and his might,
 and the wonders that he has done.

## How Do We Categorize the Parables?

Christians have sometimes sought to explain the parables by putting them into different categories. Some parables, for example, are described as parables of judgment, while others are described as parables of grace. Still other parables are sometimes distinguished as parables of the kingdom. There's some sense in the efforts, but I believe these attempts to put parables into neatly distinguished categories fall short. Why? Because, rightly understood, every one of the parables includes both judgment and grace. Is the parable of the prodigal son a parable of grace? Of course it is. Just consider the profound picture of God's unmerited favor in the father's eager embrace of his once-lost younger son. But is the same story a parable of judgment? Again, of course it is. Just consider the truth revealed about the older son. Is it a parable of the kingdom? You know the answer already; it reveals an infinitely rich picture of God's kingdom in the celebration of repentance and restoration. The father throws a joyous celebration because his son who was lost has been found, his son who was dead is now alive. Earlier in Luke 15 we are told that "there will be more joy in heaven over one sinner who repents than over ninety-nine righteous persons who need no repentance" (v. 7). There we glimpse the kingdom of heaven in the words only Jesus the Son of God could have spoken. Grace, judgment, kingdom—in every parable.

But this also means that grace and judgment can appear without being described. There is grace, the true favor of God, in being told the truth of the righteous judgment of God that is to come. And there is judgment, eternal judgment, in any rejection of grace. Attempting to categorize Jesus' parables by forming lists of parables of judgment and parables of grace is reductionistic. Every parable is a revelation of both grace and judgment, as well as a window into the kingdom of heaven. We simply need to look for the grace *and* the judgment in every parable, and understand every single parable as a revelation of the kingdom of heaven.

There have also been attempts to differentiate the parables by literary structure and length and context. We will give attention to all these issues, and more, but I will not attempt to put the parables into categories, other than to suggest commonalities of subject matter. Some of the parables seem to reveal commonalities of theme. Others seem basically to stand alone. We will take them by turn, understanding that in the truest sense, they *all* belong together as the stories Jesus told.

## Some Words of Conviction

*There is no one who comes from nowhere.* The phrase strains the English language, but that is the point—put positively, we all come from somewhere. When we interpret Holy Scripture, we all arrive with certain convictions already in place. I want to make my convictions clear, for you should know that my own doctrinal convictions will have a great deal to do with how I understand the parables of Jesus. We live in an age that is inhospitable to truth claims and subversive of doctrinal certainties. A "hermeneutic of suspicion" has long ruled in much of the academic world and now infuses the broader culture. Rather than submitting to Scripture as the Word of God, many biblical scholars submit the Bible to their own suspicions, effectively treating the Bible as human artifact and denying the divine inspiration of the text.

I take a different approach. First, I affirm the total truthfulness and trustworthiness of the Word of God. I believe that every word of Holy Scripture is breathed by God and inspired by the Holy Spirit. It is truth without any mixture of error. To doubt the Scripture is to doubt the power and character of God.

I believe that we have exactly what the Holy Spirit intended us to have in Matthew, Mark, and Luke, including the parables of Jesus and the context we are given for each of them. The biblical text reveals exactly what Jesus said, and exactly when and where he said it. This means that our interpretation must be historical and grammatical, dealing first of all with the text and context. We must also understand each parable within the unfolding story of redemption and in the flow of redemption history.

Relatedly, we must guard against the temptation to allegorize the parables, which risks both misreading the text and getting lost in details at the expense of the parable's intended effect. For centuries, the parables were buried in layer upon layer of allegorical interpretation. Claims were made, for example, that the ring put on the younger son's finger in the parable of the prodigal son represented baptism. Every detail in a parable was ransacked for a meaning pointing to something else. Actually, the ring in the parable means a ring, a symbol of sonship. Pressing it further robs the parable of its power. The Protestant

Reformers were right to point us to the plain meaning of the text. We will seek to do the same. We will look to Jesus to tell us what the parables mean.

Second, we must be clear about who Jesus Christ is and understand the parables in light of his identity. These are not just timeless stories told by a great moral teacher. These are stories told by the Son of God in human flesh. When Christ tells us of the kingdom, he speaks as King. When he warns us of the judgment that is to come, he speaks as the one who will come to earth again and judge the nations with a rod of iron. When he describes the grace of God, he speaks of the character and saving purpose of his own Father. He tells us of grace, because he *is* grace. As we learn from John 1:16–17, "From his fullness we have all received, grace upon grace. For the law was given through Moses; grace and truth came through Jesus Christ."

Finally, a word about eschatology (the branch of theology that focuses on "last things," such as our final destiny and the goal of God's redemptive work). Every parable is eschatological, pointing to the ultimate fulfillment of God's purpose and plan. Every parable starts in this world but tells us truths about the world to come. Put another way, every parable is eschatological in its horizon. I am convinced that every prophecy and promise God made concerning the end of days will be completely fulfilled in space and time and history. I believe that this expectation is a necessary foundation for understanding the parables and the promises of God. We will operate from the perspective of an "inaugurated eschatology." Jesus inaugurated the kingdom of heaven and declared that with his coming the kingdom had arrived. But the fullness of that kingdom yet awaits, and God has a purpose for continuing life in this age and assigning to Christians a work we are to do, until Christ comes again, as he surely will.

That means we are living in that time marked as already, but not yet. Christ has come and the kingdom is real. But the crucified, resurrected, and ascended Lord is coming again, and his kingdom will someday be established in its infinite fullness.

But make no mistake, Jesus Christ is the reigning Lord and King even now, our Prophet and Priest and King. As we learn from Jesus' parables, we pray that prayer the Bible teaches us to pray in the closing words of Scripture: "Come, Lord Jesus!"

## What to Expect from This Book

My prayer is that you will find in this book a doorway to encountering the power of Jesus' parables for yourself. Admittedly, we live in a different world from the world of Jesus' first-century listeners. But equipped with the lens of historical context, a little bit of attentiveness, and a heart open to the things of God, the parables are just as powerful today as they were two thousand years ago. In the chapters that follow, we will walk together through all of Jesus' parables, encountering rich, compelling truths about the kingdom of God that will change how you think and live. After all, the Word of God *is* living and active and sharper than any two-edged sword (Heb. 4:12).

But before we jump into the parables themselves, you may be wondering, "Why parables? Yes, stories are powerful ways of communicating truth—but surely Jesus had other, better options for telling people about the kingdom of heaven." If you're wondering something like that, you're not alone. The next chapter examines the time when Jesus' own disciples confronted him about his use of parables—and his answer provides the key to reading and understanding the parables today.

# 1

# Why Do You Speak to Them in Parables?

With many such parables he spoke the word to them,
as they were able to hear it. He did not speak to them
without a parable, but privately to his own disciples he
explained everything.

—MARK 4:33–34

Jesus drew large crowds as he taught and preached. Both Matthew and Mark tell us that Jesus spoke a parable nearly every time he taught. This makes perfect sense to us now. We are so familiar with the New Testament parables that we take for granted that at any given moment in Jesus' teaching ministry, he was likely to offer a parable to make a point or deliver a message.

But at the time, Jesus' use of parables confused and surprised his own disciples. One of the great gifts of the New Testament is how we can hear the disciples ask Jesus questions, and we can hear Jesus respond. The disciples, puzzled by Jesus' parables and wishing he would speak more straightforwardly, came right out and asked Jesus, "Why do you speak to them in parables?" (Matt. 13:10).

The context of the disciples' question is vital. Jesus had just shared with the crowd the parable of the sower. The preceding chapter (Matt. 12) describes a growing excitement in Galilee. Crowds were building, drawn both to the presence of Jesus and to the prospect of conflict. The Pharisees had recently confronted Jesus and his disciples in a wheat field on a Sabbath day, charging them with violating the Sabbath by picking grain. Jesus declared himself to be Lord of the Sabbath and pointed out that God had created the Sabbath for man, not man for the Sabbath. This infuriated the Pharisees further, and ever since then they had been doing their best to box Jesus into a corner and show their authority over him.

The conflict escalated until the Pharisees confronted Jesus in a synagogue on another Sabbath day, where they presented a man with a withered hand to Jesus and asked him, "Is it lawful to heal on the Sabbath?" (Matt. 12:10). This question was both a challenge and a trap. Their intention was to put Jesus in a lose-lose situation. Jesus could either refuse to heal the man (striking a blow to Jesus' popularity and credibility) or he could heal the man (thus breaking the Sabbath according to the Pharisees' logic). Of course, Jesus turned the tables once again on the Pharisees, pointing out that they would have the common sense to understand that an animal in trouble should be rescued on the Sabbath day—and they could all agree that God considers human beings of infinitely greater value than animals. Then he simply did what only the Son of God could do: he healed the man's hand.

On that crucial Sabbath day, right in the synagogue in front of the gathered crowd, Jesus' shrewd response to the Pharisees' challenge had revealed them to be uncaring legalists who did not understand the kingdom of God. Furthermore, by restoring the man's withered hand, he revealed himself to be the Son of God.

The Pharisees' response was swift—and would eventually prove deadly. As Matthew tells us, they "went out and conspired against him, how to destroy him" (v. 14). But on that day, Jesus continued performing signs and miracles that pointed inescapably to his identity as both the Messiah and the Son of God. No one else could do such things.

Predictably, the crowd kept growing—and growing and growing. By the time chapter 13 opens, Jesus had gone out of the house to the Sea of Galilee, where the crowd had grown so large that he had to get into a boat to create enough distance to be able to speak to everyone. The eager listeners pressed to the shoreline to hear Jesus teach from the boat, and this is when he told them the parable of the sower.

That sets the stage for the disciples asking Jesus, "Why do you speak to them in parables?" The context helps us see that the disciples expected Jesus to speak more directly about himself. They hoped he would publicly claim his Messianic identity and speak openly about his divine nature and mission. But, as we read in the Gospel of John, Jesus knew that his "hour had not yet come" (7:30; 8:20). The disciples knew who Jesus was, and the confrontations with the Pharisees and the series of healings and miracles made obvious Jesus' divine nature and power. But when Jesus sat in the boat and spoke to the vast crowd, he told them a story. A parable. No wonder the disciples were puzzled. It hardly seemed like the right time for a parable, and a parable about a farmer at that!

When the disciples asked Jesus why he spoke in parables, they were asking more than they knew—and Jesus' answer gave them far more than they expected: "To you it has been given to know the secrets of the kingdom of heaven, but to them it has not been given. For to the one who has, more will be given, and he will have an abundance, but from the one who has not, even what he has will be taken away. This is why I speak to them in parables, because seeing they do not see, and hearing they do not hear, nor do they understand" (Matt. 13:11–13).

Jesus told them that, in an incredibly important sense, the world is divided into two groups: those who hear and understand the parables, and those who hear but do not understand. The Gospel of Mark underlines this divide when Jesus said to the disciples, "To you has been given the secret of the kingdom of God, but for those outside, everything is in parables" (4:11).

The disciples must have been shocked by Jesus' answer, and if we are honest, we will sense that same shocking power today. The parables simultaneously reveal and hide. They divide their hearers into two worlds. In one world a parable makes known the secret of the kingdom of God. But in the second world a parable remains only a parable, nothing more.

Now we see more clearly what is at stake in the parables and why Jesus used them virtually every time he taught. It turns out that our *response* to the parables reveals everything important about us, with eternal consequences. Every one of the parables is an explosive disclosure of the kingdom of heaven, so if we listen to a parable and hear only a story, something is wrong.

That brings us to Jesus' comments about the one who already has receiving even greater abundance, and the one who has not eventually having nothing at all. He means that whoever understands the parable and receives the Word of God will grow and receive an increase. But the one who hears the parable and refuses to hear and see its true message gains nothing. Eventually he loses even a basic interest in the parable—and in the kingdom of God.

The seed sown by the sower in this parable is the gospel—the word of the kingdom (v. 18). The parable is telling us about the kingdom of heaven, and the key to understanding God's kingdom and rule is understanding the *gospel*—the good news that God is bringing salvation to sinners through his own Son, through his death on the cross and his resurrection from the dead. Salvation comes to those who believe in Christ as the Son of God and repent of their sins. For, as we have heard, "the kingdom of God is at hand" (Mark 1:15).

This is why some hearers hear only a story, while others, upon hearing the same parable, hear the gospel and understand the secrets of the kingdom of God. Jesus' answer also points to a deep spiritual reality that underlies the experience of the church—and especially the experience of preaching and teaching the Word of God: Those who hear the message of the kingdom in the parables grow in their faith. They become faithful and maturing disciples. To the one who has understanding, more will be given. Growth comes and comes again.

So it is with the preaching and teaching of the Word of God and the way it functions in the lives of believers today. We hear the Word, receive the Word, obey the Word, and through this "ordinary means of grace" God brings extraordinary, even supernatural, spiritual growth, leading to the progressive sanctification of the believer and greater faithfulness. By the ministry of the Word of God, the Holy Spirit works inwardly to conform the believer to the image of Christ. To the one who has, more will be given, and he will have an abundance. This is such great, good news.

Conversely, those who hear the parable and hear only a story may exhibit curiosity at first. But mere curiosity about the gospel, the things of God, or the kingdom of heaven will not last. Superficial interest in spiritual truth simply evaporates. For those who have not, even the little they have will eventually be taken away.

These two principles, which Jesus provided in his answer to the disciples' question, are incredibly clarifying. But Jesus pressed even deeper, indicating to the disciples that they were witnessing in the dual responses to Jesus' parables and miracles the fulfillment of the prophet Isaiah's words:

> "'You will indeed hear but never understand,
>
> and you will indeed see but never perceive.'
>
> For this people's heart has grown dull,
>
> and with their ears they can barely hear,
>
> and their eyes they have closed,
>
> lest they should see with their eyes
>
> and hear with their ears
>
> and understand with their heart
>
> and turn, and I would heal them."
>
> (MATT. 13:14–15)

Isaiah towers over the history of Israel as perhaps its greatest prophet. During his time as a prophet, Isaiah saw the Lord high and lifted up. He saw the glory of the Lord fill the temple, and he heard and saw the seraphim as they flew in declaring, "Holy, holy, holy is the LORD of hosts; the whole earth is full of his glory!" (Isa. 6:3).

Isaiah experienced the depth of his own sinfulness as he beheld God's holiness. Then he experienced the grace of God as his sins were atoned for. Then and only then did Isaiah hear that divine call to be God's prophet: "Whom shall I send, and who will go for us?" (v. 8). Answering the call, Isaiah famously answered, "Here am I! Send me" (v. 8). What immediately follows is shocking. Isaiah was charged with warning the people that they would hear but not understand. They would see but not perceive. Their ears would be heavy, their eyes blind, and their hearts dull.

But there's also promise in Isaiah's mission. There is hope. Some would truly see and hear. And they would return to God, repenting and experiencing healing.

By alluding to Isaiah, Jesus' answer to the disciples (and through them, the church) reveals that there is both danger and promise in the preaching of the gospel. There is both grace and judgment in the parables, and in all preaching. It comes down to whether or not we truly *hear* and truly *see*. If we do, hearing and seeing will be demonstrated in obeying Christ and repenting of our sins and returning to God—the very picture of the saving power of the gospel.

Jesus told his disciples that he spoke in parables because, even as the parables powerfully disclose kingdom truth, the response to the parables (and to the preaching of the gospel itself) reveals the true condition of the human heart. Hearing means life. Refusing to hear means death. As Jesus told the crowd: "He who has ears, let him hear" (Matt. 13:9).

And yet, there is even more to the matter. Jesus assured his disciples, "But blessed are your eyes, for they see, and your ears, for they hear. For truly, I say to you, many prophets and righteous people longed to see what you see, and did not see it, and to hear what you hear and did not hear it" (vv. 16–17).

But how did they hear and see when others had failed? Were they more perceptive? Were they more spiritually sensitive? Should we give them credit for hearing and seeing the truth? What about us—can we open our own ears and eyes? Can we soften our own hearts to receive these messages of the kingdom?

The answer is no. We have no such power. And yet, Jesus made clear that we do bear responsibility to see, to hear, and to believe.

Here we come face-to-face with one of the greatest and most humbling truths of the Bible. We stand at the intersection of God's sovereignty and human responsibility. But the sovereignty of God is absolute, primary, and fundamental. The starting point of all Christian theology is the one true, living God, the triune God in three persons—Father, Son, and Holy Spirit—the omnipotent and sovereign King. God's absolute rule—his sovereignty—extends throughout the cosmos and through the human heart.

Look with me at verse 16. Jesus did not tell the disciples that they were high achievers on a spiritual scale. He told them that their eyes were blessed, for they were allowed to see. Their ears were blessed, because they were allowed to hear. As the New Testament teaches us, salvation comes only through the miracle of regeneration. Only the quickening power of the Holy Spirit can open hearts that sin has made dull. Only God's work of regeneration can explain how ears now hear and eyes now see—and hearts now receive the gospel.

Behind Jesus' answer to the disciples' question is the doctrine of election and the sovereign power of God. Nothing less—and nothing else—can explain why some people hear the gospel and others do not. Why some see, while others are blind. Jesus told his disciples what all Christians desperately need to hear. The parables, like the gospel itself, come as both grace and judgment. To those who see and hear, who believe and repent, who trust and obey, there is infinite grace— even the saving grace of God. As John Bunyan put it in the title of his nineteenth-century classic, this is "grace abounding to the chief of sinners."

But the parables—and the gospel—come as judgment for those who will not see, will not hear, will not believe. For them, every word they will ever hear from Jesus looms over them as everlasting judgment.

The apostle Paul wrote, "For by grace you have been saved through faith. And this is not your own doing; it is the gift of God, not a result of works, so that no one may boast" (Eph. 2:8–9). We bear the responsibility to believe the gospel, to trust Christ, to profess our faith, and to hear and obey the Word of God. But our ability to do so—even our desire to do so—comes only by the grace of God and only by the mercy of Christ.

Our task is to remember these truths as we consider Jesus' parables, as we hear the holy Scriptures, any verse, any time. We pray for eyes ever more open, ears ever more eager, hearts ever more faithful. I invite you to come with me to the parables of Jesus, looking for more and more, so that we may glorify God ever more greatly.

He who has ears to hear, let him hear.

# 2

# Hearts Ready to
# Receive the Word

## THE PARABLE OF THE SOWER

Then the LORD said to Samuel, "Behold, I am about to
do a thing in Israel at which the two ears of everyone
who hears it will tingle."

—1 SAMUEL 3:11

That same day Jesus went out of the house and sat beside the
sea. And great crowds gathered about him, so that he got into
a boat and sat down. And the whole crowd stood on the beach.
And he told them many things in parables, saying: "A sower
went out to sow. And as he sowed, some seeds fell along the
path, and the birds came and devoured them. Other seeds
fell on rocky ground, where they did not have much soil, and
immediately they sprang up, since they had no depth of soil,

but when the sun rose they were scorched. And since they had
no root, they withered away. Other seeds fell among thorns,
and the thorns grew up and choked them. Other seeds fell on
good soil and produced grain, some a hundredfold, some sixty,
some thirty. He who has ears, let him hear." (Matt. 13:1–9)

Oddly enough, one of the great challenges for the Christian church
is knowing the difference between a church and a crowd. It should
perhaps reassure us that Jesus' disciples faced the same challenge.

A massive crowd had gathered to hear Jesus speak. Matthew tells
us "the whole crowd stood on the beach." Jesus had much to say to
them, but Matthew tells us that "he told them many things in parables,"
consistent with what we know was Jesus' usual practice.

"A sower went out to sow," Jesus told them. Galilee (and most of the
world) at that time was agricultural. The growing of food was one of
the most visible tasks of civilization, second only to the task of raising
the next generation of children. Sowers of seed were everywhere, and
no task could have been more clearly understood than sowing seed.
Given the context, a sower may have been in sight even as Jesus told the
parable. In any event, the parable began with what every hearer could
see and understand. The sower went out to sow.

As this sower sowed the seeds, some of the precious seeds fell in the
path, some on rocky ground, some among thorns, and some in good,
productive soil. The results were predictable. Given the types of soil
described, no one could have expected a different outcome.

The parable reveals a picture of the generous, widespread, un-
discriminating sowing of seed. The sower presented the seed to the
pathway, but no seed penetrated the surface at all, as the ground was
utterly unreceptive. Furthermore, the birds came and took the seed

away. Go ahead, try this for yourself. The birds will come and take the seed and it will be as if you had never sown any seed at all.

Some seed fell on rocky ground. The soil was thin and shallow. The seed was received by the ground, but only at a superficial level. Close to the sun, the seeds sprang immediately to life in the shallow soil. But woe to the farmer who finds encouragement in this soil. The early sprouts are an empty promise. Eventually, the heat of the sun becomes the problem. As the sprouts head for the warmth of the sun, the absence of soil means that the root cannot draw enough nourishment, leaving it weak and vulnerable. The sun scorches the plant and it dies. The sprouts simply wither away.

Still other seed fell among thorns. Again, this is something we can all picture. We call some plants weeds because, infuriatingly for anyone who has tried his or her hand at gardening, they choke the life out of what we are trying to grow. Among the thorns, the seeds had little chance. The weeds choked the sprouts in the thorn-infested soil. So far, among the seeds sown on the path, on rocky ground, and among the thorns, no hope for a harvest.

Everything changed when Jesus shared that some seed fell in good soil. Now, finally, we see the promise of a harvest. The seed in the good soil brings forth life and produces a harvest of grain. Sometimes the harvest is thirtyfold, sometimes sixtyfold, sometimes even a hundredfold.

Now, let's be honest. Those who are already familiar with the parables know that Jesus explained this parable to his disciples. But let's try our best to deal with the parable as if we have not heard Jesus explain it.

Probably no one thought that Jesus was offering mere agricultural advice or observation. The crowd had not been gathering to hear Jesus give the daily farm report. No, they were looking for Jesus to say or do something that would decisively disclose the plan and purpose of

God. They were right to expect this. And yet, did anyone realize that the parable they had just heard was that powerful message? Did anyone who heard the parable get a glimpse of the kingdom?

Remember that Jesus told the disciples that some would see and others would not. It is reasonable to expect that the disciples themselves understood something of what Jesus was revealing about the kingdom in the parable—even before he explained it. After all, before he offered the explanation of the parable, Jesus told the disciples, "Blessed are your eyes, for they see, and your ears, for they hear" (v. 16).

This parable is the key that unlocks all the parables. In a real sense, this parable explains the nature of Christian preaching and evangelism. It points us to different patterns of response to the gospel of Jesus Christ and to the Word of God.

Some of the crowd hear the Word and it has no effect on them whatsoever. Some hear and respond superficially, but without any real commitment. Others want to receive the gospel in its benefits, but they are ultimately more committed to other priorities. At last, some hear— truly hear—the gospel, receive the grace and mercy of God, and are utterly transformed. The proof of this transformation is described as a magnificent harvest of grain. In every case the seed is the same. The difference is found in the soils, not in the seed.

As we saw in the previous chapter, this is the parable that led the disciples to ask Jesus why he spoke in parables. After all, why use a word picture when he could have simply said something like, "Look, not everyone is going to believe that I am the Messiah, the Son of God. Not everyone is going to believe in me and trust and be saved. Not everyone who claims to be my disciple will turn out to be authentic. Some are going to fall away. We're going to see people who turn out to love the world more than they love me. But there will be true believers who hear and believe and are saved. They will go on to live lives of faithfulness and fruitfulness that will reveal the spectacular grace and mercy of the Father. That's just the way it is."

In effect, Jesus *did* say something like that to the disciples when he explained the parable in verses 18–23. But never lose sight of the fact that Jesus *first* told them the parable. Think of it this way: We (and the disciples) remember these truths even now (and remember them so powerfully) precisely because Jesus first told us the parable. We can *see* the sower, and we can *see* the soils. The explanation is further grace— but it all started with the parable.

Remember that Mark told us that Jesus told his parables to crowds, but "privately to his own disciples he explained everything" (Mark 4:34).

In the case of the parable of the sower, we get to overhear Jesus explain the parable. In between the parable and the explanation, Jesus answered the question of why he spoke in parables, and we need to hold closely to something Jesus told the disciples in that passage. Jesus made repeated references to hearing and seeing, but in every case the ultimate issue was the human heart. Jesus had quoted Isaiah, who was told by God that "this people's heart has grown dull." They would find salvation and the forgiveness of sins only if they would "see with their eyes and hear with their ears and understand with their heart and turn, and I would heal them" (Matt. 13:15).

There are people with perfectly good eyes who will not see the truth. There are people with perfectly good ears who will not hear the truth. But the eyes and ears simply point to the real issue—the heart.

Throughout the Bible, the heart represents the innermost person— the you that lives within. It is the seat of our self-consciousness, character, decision-making, and emotions. Just think of what we find in Proverbs 23. Solomon yearned for his son's heart to be wise: "My son, if your heart is wise, my heart too will be glad" (Prov. 23:15). He then spoke of the heart as his "inmost being" (v. 16). His son is warned against letting his heart envy sinners (v. 16). The son is admonished to "direct your heart in the way" (v. 19), meaning the way of God. He called for his son to "give me your heart" and thus to avoid prostitutes and sexual sin (v. 26). He warned his son against the dangers of wine, advising, "your heart [will] utter perverse things" (v. 33).

Tellingly, the prophet Ezekiel described redemption beautifully as a new heart. Speaking through his prophet, God said: "And I will give you a new heart, and a new spirit I will put within you. And I will remove the heart of stone from your flesh and give you a heart of flesh" (Ezek. 36:26).

So it turns out that the condition of the heart means *everything* when it comes to receiving the Word of God, just as the condition of the soil means everything when it comes to the fate of the seed in Jesus' parable. In short, the four soils illustrate four types of hearts, and the four hearts reveal four different patterns of response to the Word of God.

## The Hard Soil = The Rejecting Heart

The diagnosis of a hardened heart is well known from the Old Testament. God told Isaiah that Israel's heart was dull. Pharoah's heart, in the account of the exodus, is described as hardened, totally resistant to God. The prophet Samuel asked the children of Israel, "Why should you harden your hearts as the Egyptians and Pharaoh hardened their hearts?" (1 Sam. 6:6).

In the New Testament we see a hardened heart as both a diagnosis and a warning. Paul described those who have rejected God by stating: "They are darkened in their understanding, alienated from the life of God because of the ignorance that is in them, due to their hardness of heart" (Eph. 4:18). In the book of Hebrews, believers are warned: "Do not harden your hearts" (3:8). We also find this bracing word: "Take care, brothers, lest there be in any of you an evil, unbelieving heart, leading you to fall away from the living God" (v. 12).

We had better pay close attention to Jesus' explanation of the soil on the hardened path: "When anyone hears the word of the kingdom and does not understand it, the evil one comes and snatches away what has been sown in his heart" (Matt. 13:19).

The German preacher Helmut Thielicke described certain hearts as like asphalt. They are so hard that *nothing* can penetrate them. Jesus used the vivid description of a hardened pathway to indict hearts that simply *refuse* to hear. In a very real sense, they *cannot* hear for they have developed an insensitivity to all spiritual truth. They reject God and hate the gospel.

In our increasingly secular age, we encounter more and more people who refuse to hear the gospel. The Bible will keep us from any assumption that this is a new response to the Word of God, but in the present age an especially secular generation appears eager to slam the door and reject the gospel outright. With the decline of a Christian conscience in society at large, we're seeing a new aggressiveness in the secular spirit.

But hearts have been hardened since Adam and Eve were expelled from the garden of Eden. In Matthew 13:19, Jesus attributed the loss of knowledge to the work of "the evil one," who "snatches away what has been sown in his heart." In Mark's telling of the parable, Jesus referred to Satan by name. Satan hates the gospel and loves a hardened heart.

Some years ago, I had a conversation with a pastor who had bravely preached the gospel to a congregation in London for decades. I asked him how England had changed over the course of his ministry. He told me that the most significant change came in the loss of what he called a "Sunday school conscience." He meant that generations of unbelief had produced a society filled with people who had not just rejected the gospel—they had even lost the vestigial benefits of a biblical conscience and morality. They had forgotten the moral foundations of their own society. As Jesus warned, to those who have not, even what they have will be taken away.

## The Shallow Soil = The Superficial Heart

The appearance of new life does not always mean new life. One frightening response to the gospel is an eager acceptance that eventually reveals itself to be a superficial commitment. If you've been in the church for any length of time, you've almost certainly encountered people who claimed a Christian commitment and showed great enthusiasm for the things of God, but whose commitment faltered and eventually disappeared.

Those who genuinely come to faith in Jesus Christ will persevere. As the Westminster Confession of Faith states succinctly and truly: "They whom God hath accepted in his Beloved, effectively called and sanctified by his Spirit, can neither totally nor finally fall away from the state of grace; but shall certainly persevere therein to the end, and be eternally saved."[1]

One of the most precious passages of Scripture is found in the Gospel of John, where Jesus stated: "All that the Father gives me will come to me, and whoever comes to me I will never cast out. For I have come down from heaven, not to do my own will but the will of him who sent me. And this is the will of him who sent me, that I should lose nothing of all that he has given me, but raise it up at the last day" (6:37–39). Christ will lose nothing—he will lose *no one.*

But the fact remains—and this is a difficult truth—that false believers will appear, even as false prophets have appeared throughout the history of God's people. Initial enthusiasm does not always indicate lifelong commitment.

Jesus spoke of the superficial believer as one who "hears the word and immediately receives it with joy" (Matt. 13:20). At first glance, this is exactly what we are looking for—an eager and enthusiastic response to the gospel message and the Word of God. But enthusiasm can simultaneously reveal and conceal. It takes time to mature in Christ and grow in grace. Only faithfulness over time produces fruitfulness.

Jesus described the superficial heart as having no root. This is similar to the picture he provided in the Gospel of John of true believers as fruitful branches and false believers as unfruitful branches. No root means no real life, "and when tribulation or persecution arises on account of the word, immediately he falls away" (v. 21).

Our Lord's explicit mention of tribulation or persecution *on account of the word* is crucial. One way of describing the superficial heart is to point to the reality of "nominal Christians" or "cultural Christianity." In cultures historically shaped by Christianity, identifying as a Christian and joining a church have been cultural expectations. To use one helpful category, individuals gained social capital, including social respectability, by identifying as a Christian and attending Christian services. More recently, the cultural tables have been turned. Under the pressure of an increasingly secular culture, the social benefit of Christian identification decreases. Under conditions of more overt hostility to Christianity, those who identify as Christians, claim the name of Christ, and are active in their involvement in a gospel church may actually *lose* social capital rather than gain it.

By now, there is abundant evidence that the process of secularization has rapidly accelerated in the United States. Recent studies of church membership and Christian self-identification reveal a marked decrease in both church membership and involvement. We are witnessing the evaporation of nominal Christianity—cultural Christianity—in just one generation.

Put bluntly, the pressures of the age indicate that much of what had constituted Christian commitment in the general population is exceedingly thin. Of course, persecution has been a real threat to Christians in many parts of the world since the time of the apostles. For some believers, the threat has been not the loss of social capital but the loss of one's head. False faith is revealed under the glare of persecution—like the plant that withers under the noonday sun because it has no depth of soil. As evangelical pastor Adrian Rogers used to say, "The faith that fizzles at the finish was faulty at the first." Jesus made that truth clear in the parable of the sower.

## The Weed-Infested Soil = The Unfruitful Heart

One of the most consistent teachings of Scripture is the requirement of fruitfulness. Jesus cursed the fig tree, precisely because it bore no fruit (Matt. 21:18–22; Mark 11:12–14). In the first psalm, the godly believer is described as "like a tree planted by streams of water that yields its fruit in its season" (Ps. 1:3).

It's a beautiful picture: Jesus is the true vine and we are his branches. Branches connected to the lifegiving vine yield fruit. Unfruitful branches reveal a faulty connection to the vine—and they are cut off. Jesus said: "I am the true vine, and my Father is the vinedresser. Every branch in me that does not bear fruit he takes away, and every branch that does bear fruit he prunes, that it may bear more fruit" (John 15:1–2).

Jesus explained this third soil, and this third pattern of response to the gospel, as one who appears to hear the word but never produces fruit.

Some of the most dangerous confusions in today's Christianity are just contemporary versions of age-old heresies and false gospels. The gospel of Christ is the gospel of God's grace. It promises salvation to those who believe in Christ as Savior and repent of their sins. It is premised upon God's saving acts in the death, burial, and resurrection of the Lord Jesus Christ. The Bible makes clear that there is nothing we can do to earn our salvation. It is all grace—grace from the beginning to the end. Salvation is entirely God's gracious gift, and we contribute *nothing*. This is why the Reformers rightly stressed salvation by grace alone through faith alone, on the merits of Christ alone. The gospel is not the gospel without each of these *alones*.

But, even as the faith that saves is faith alone, the faith that saves never comes alone. In other words good works always follow salvation. But the order is essential. Saving faith is followed by the demonstration of good works. The regenerate Christian begins to bear fruit and over the course of Christian faithfulness and maturity bears ever more fruit.

Jesus did not say that if we obey we will be saved, but he did emphatically state that if we are truly saved, we will obey him. Jesus told the disciples, "Whoever has my commandments and keeps them, he it is who loves me" (John 14:21). Further, Christ explained: "If anyone loves me, he will keep my word, and my Father will love him, and we will come to him and make our home with him. Whoever does not love me does not keep my words" (vv. 23–24).

Jesus warned specifically about "the cares of the world and the deceitfulness of riches" that threatened to choke the word (Matt. 13:22). Again, Jesus was presenting such a powerful picture. The word is choked by materialism and other worldly temptations. Jesus' diagnosis so many years ago remains true now: the cares and temptations of life in the world are soul-killing unless they are countered by gospel commitment and faithfulness to Christ.

The great temptation is to believe that we can have both the promises of salvation in Christ and ultimate earthly satisfaction. There is no such satisfaction to be found on earth, but history is replete with the stories of those who thought they could have both but ended up with neither.

False gospels today include prosperity theology, which presents the gospel as a highway to health and wealth, and those who promise a salvation that requires no obedience. As Jesus made abundantly and consistently clear, the gospel requires our obedience to Christ—including obedience to the first command to believe in the Lord Jesus Christ and to be saved. Without Christ there is no fruitfulness, and the absence of fruitfulness means the absence of life. In truth, there could be no more severe indictment of a human heart.

## The Good Soil = The Infinite Power of the Word of God in the Obedient Heart

The climax of the parable is the seed exploding in growth in producing a harvest. This harvest takes place when the Word of God is heard and believed and obeyed—producing a harvest of godliness and faithfulness. Here we see the good soil—good because it fulfills the purpose for which it was created.

Note carefully: The power is in the *seed*, in the Word of God, not in the soil. The soil *receives* the good seed of the gospel. The Word of God comes in saving power and authority and transforms lives. The dead are made alive, the blind see, sinners are redeemed by the blood of the Lamb. Sins are forgiven, the Father's love is freely given, and the glory of God is revealed.

Jesus explained this truth plainly: "As for what was sown on good soil, this is the one who hears the word and understands it. He indeed bears fruit and yields, in one case a hundredfold, in another sixty, and in another thirty" (v. 23). The harvest is unprecedented and supernatural—and that is the point.

## The Ministry of the Word

Never, ever, underestimate the power of the Word of God, the power of the gospel of Jesus Christ. In this parable, and in the entire passage that includes both Jesus' answer to the disciples' question and his explanation of the parable itself, the great emphasis is upon the fact that the Christian church is assigned a ministry of the Word. Our assignment is to take the gospel to the ends of the earth and make disciples. Our task is, as Paul instructed Timothy, to preach the word in season and out of season (2 Tim. 4:1–2).

Christian ministry is not about technique and it is certainly not about the latest fads or glittering programs. It is about the ministry of the Word—most importantly, the preaching and teaching of the Word of God. Gospel ministry and the preaching of the Word of God are not just an initial strategy—there is no Plan B. God's glory is in the preaching of his Word, and the evidence of the Word's power is a harvest of transformed lives.

Only the Word of God can penetrate the sinful human heart and its hardened defenses. As Hebrews 4:12 tells us, "The word of God is living and active, sharper than any two-edged sword, piercing to the division of soul and of spirit, of joints and of marrow, and discerning the thoughts and intentions of the heart." Nothing but the Word of God can do this work, but God's Word *does this work*. Such is the power of the Word of God.

# 3

# The Children of Light and the Children of Darkness

## THE PARABLE OF THE WEEDS

For at one time you were darkness, but now you are light in the Lord. Walk as children of light.

—EPHESIANS 5:8

Again Jesus spoke to them, saying, "I am the light of the world. Whoever follows me will not walk in darkness, but will have the light of life."

—JOHN 8:12

But if we walk in the light, as he is in the light, we have fellowship with one another, and the blood of Jesus his Son cleanses us from all sin.

—1 JOHN 1:7

Do not be unequally yoked with unbelievers. For what partnership has righteousness with lawlessness? Or what fellowship has light with darkness?

—2 CORINTHIANS 6:14

He put another parable before them, saying, "The kingdom of heaven may be compared to a man who sowed good seed in his field, but while his men were sleeping, his enemy came and sowed weeds among the wheat and went away. So when the plants came up and bore grain, then the weeds appeared also. And the servants of the master of the house came and said to him, 'Master, did you not sow good seed in your field? How then does it have weeds?' He said to them, 'An enemy has done this.' So the servants said to him, 'Then do you want us to go and gather them?' But he said, 'No, lest in gathering the weeds you root up the wheat along with them. Let both grow together until the harvest, and at harvest time I will tell the reapers, "Gather the weeds first and bind them in bundles to be burned, but gather the wheat into my barn."'" (Matt. 13:24–30)

We now understand that Jesus used agricultural stories because we can all relate to them. He spoke in parables because these transformative stories catch us by surprise, converting something expected into something very unexpected.

The agricultural pattern of life is as familiar to us as the seasons. Even those of us who are not farmers know enough to get the point when we read Jesus' parable about a sower and different kinds of soil. We also understand something about weeds, which are the bane of every farmer's or gardener's existence. In the parable of the sower, Jesus told us that weeds choke the good seed in the stony ground, representing a superficial heart. In any context, weeds are the enemy of the crop—and of the farmer. Left alone, they can quickly take over a field. But Jesus had a specific message for us when he turned to weeds again. In this case, the weeds had been sown among the wheat. As familiar as the image of wheat and weeds would have been to his first hearers, Jesus turned the parable in a direction they could never have expected.

The story appears quite straightforward. Jesus compared the kingdom of heaven to a man who sowed good seed in his field, only to have his enemy come and sow weeds among the wheat. Jesus explained that the farmer's workmen were sleeping, and as they slept the enemy came and did evil work, intentionally contaminating the field with weeds.

R. T. France has shared that the weed in this case is almost certainly darnel, a weed that looks so much like wheat that distinguishing one from the other is only possible when the grains appear on the stalk. If one were to plant the seeds together, it would be virtually impossible to separate the wheat from the weeds until the time of harvest. During the time of the Roman Empire, planting darnel in a wheat field as an act of revenge was so common that the Romans had to criminalize it.[1]

Darnel is not only an inferior wheat lookalike, it is a poisonous grain. Left with the wheat, it will contaminate the entire harvest. Jesus shared that when the servants of the master saw that the weeds had contaminated the crop they went to their master and asked if they should go and immediately pluck the weeds out from among the wheat. But the wise farmer understood that this course of action, due to the similarity of the two plants, would risk destroying the entire crop. Instead, he told them to allow the wheat and the weeds to grow together until the time of harvest. Then and only then would he tell the reapers, "Gather the weeds first and bind them in bundles to be burned, but gather the wheat into my barn."

How are we to understand this parable? What is the field? Is it the church? Is it the world?

Thankfully, this is one of the rare occasions when the biblical author provided for us Jesus' explanation of his own parable. Once again we see exactly what we saw in the parable of the sower: Jesus told a massive crowd the parable, but he explained it only to his disciples in private.

Jesus' explanation runs as follows: The sower of the good seed is none other than the Son of Man—Jesus himself. The good seed represents Jesus' own disciples and followers. And in verse 38, Jesus explained that the field is the world. This is of crucial importance. If the field is the world (not the church, as some interpreters have suggested), the weeds sown among the wheat do not signify a mixed church. Rather, they illustrate the place of the church in the world. The good seeds, Jesus explained, are the sons of the kingdom, planted by Jesus. The weeds are the sons of the Evil One, planted by the devil. Extending the story, Jesus said, "The harvest is the end of the age, and the reapers are angels. Just as the weeds are gathered and burned with fire, so will it be at the end of the age" (vv. 39–40). At the end of the age, the Son of Man will himself send the angels, and they will gather out of the world all sin and all causes of sin. Lawbreakers will face judgment, like weeds thrown in a fiery furnace. The nature of that judgment is clear, for Jesus said that in that place "there will be weeping and gnashing of teeth" (v. 42). But then Jesus pointed to the climactic conclusion of the parable: "Then the righteous will shine like the sun in the kingdom of their Father. He who has ears, let him hear" (v. 43).

Throughout church history, various interpreters have tried to use this parable as a way of explaining that the church is, in essence, an intentionally mixed assembly until the day of judgment. If that interpretation is correct, the church could not be understood as the regenerate assembly of those who have come to saving knowledge of the Lord Jesus Christ and are following him as his disciples, but rather a mixed body of those who are both faithful and faithless, regenerate and dead in their sins and trespasses. Thankfully, Jesus' own explanation sets the record straight, with the remainder of the New Testament writings declaring in unity that the church is the blood-bought assembly of the saints, responsible for stewarding truth, ministering the gospel, and exercising church discipline for the increasing holiness of believers. The church is to be made up of professing believers who are gathered together in a covenant of mutual accountability to the Lord Jesus Christ, displaying the kingdom of God on earth until it is fully realized when Christ returns.

One of the pressing questions that early Christians faced, as recorded later in the New Testament, was the apparent delay of Christ's return. As months turned into years and decades, believers wondered when the kingdom of God would arrive in its fullness. As we know, God is in sovereign control of the entire span of human history and all that will take place in the coming of Christ will be fulfilled exactly according to his sovereign plan. But even during Jesus' earthly ministry, his own disciples constantly asked him if now was the time when he would inaugurate the kingdom in its fullness. After the resurrection, as they were with Jesus in the upper room in the first chapter of Acts, the disciples pressed him again: "Lord, will you at this time restore the kingdom to Israel?" (v. 6). Jesus answered the disciples by telling them that the church was to remain in the world in order to be his witnesses in this age. In fact, the Holy Spirit would come upon them, empowering them to be his witnesses "in Jerusalem and in all Judea and Samaria, and to the ends of the earth" (v. 8).

The distinction between the church and the world drawn by

Jesus in the parable of the weeds is described even more graphically elsewhere in the New Testament. In the Gospel of Matthew, Jesus repeatedly referred to the sinful society of his age—and by extension, the sinful society of every age until he comes—as "an evil and adulterous generation" (Matt. 12:39; 16:4). In Matthew 17:17, Jesus told his audience that they are an "unbelieving and perverse generation" (NIV), echoing the Old Testament's description of Israel in a moment of rebellion as a "wicked and perverse generation" (Deut. 32:5 DRA). Similarly, Paul told believers in Philippi that they live "in the midst of a crooked and perverse generation" (Phil. 2:15).

Jesus spoke of his own people as the children of light, in sharp contrast to the "crooked" children of darkness. The apostle Paul used the same contrast when he exhorted Christians, "Do all things without grumbling or disputing, that you may be blameless and innocent, children of God without blemish in the midst of a crooked and twisted generation, among whom you shine as lights in the world" (Phil. 2:14–15). Similarly, in 1 Thessalonians 5:5, Paul reminded believers, "For you are all children of light, children of the day. We are not of the night or of the darkness."

Just think about the contrast between light and darkness. This is the contrast Jesus described between his people and the world in which the church is situated until he comes. In the parable we are considering, Jesus referred to wheat and weeds as two different realities with eternal significance. The wheat is the seed sown by Christ himself, whereas the weeds are the seeds sown by none other than the devil. All this points, of course, to a judgment that is to come, and Jesus made clear that that judgment will be devastating for the children of the devil. Just as weeds would be thrown into a furnace for destruction, so will those who belong to the devil himself.

When considering this stark contrast between light and darkness, wheat and weeds, children of God and children of the devil, keep in mind that the very Lord Jesus Christ who spoke this parable described himself as "the light of the world" (John 8:12). Since Jesus is himself the Light of the World, illuminating all who come to believe in him, his believers are also sons and daughters of light.

The metaphor of light is among the most powerful and consistent in all of Scripture. In God's work of creation, the separation of light from darkness is one of the most crucial moments in the creation of the entire cosmos. The difference between light and darkness is the difference between knowledge and ignorance, between life and death. So when the New Testament refers to believers as the children of light in the midst of the children of darkness, we immediately understand the power of this metaphor. It situates the church as the people of Christ within a culture that is not spiritually neutral, but antagonistic. There is no third seed and there is no third spiritual condition. Every single human being on planet Earth is at this moment either a child of light or a child of darkness, belonging either to Christ or to the devil. The parable of the weeds is one of the most powerful revelations of this truth, but it is not alone in its proclamation.

Writing to the early church, John spoke of the children of God as opposed to the children of the devil: "By this it is evident who are the children of God, and who are the children of the devil: whoever does not practice righteousness is not of God, nor is the one who does not love his brother" (1 John 3:10). In other words, there are distinguishing marks of the children of God as contrasted with the children of the devil. The children of God practice righteousness.

Furthermore, the church is set apart by the way they live, called to be holy even as God is holy (1 Peter 1:15–16). In his first epistle, Peter described the church as "elect exiles of the Dispersion" (1:1). This is such an important word for us. The church's exile status in the world is exactly what will bring glory to God and is exactly what God intends to be the experience of the church in this age. Witness is the central role of the church, and the elect exiles are secure in the purposes of God, "in the sanctification of the Spirit, for obedience to Jesus Christ and for sprinkling with his blood" (v. 2). The exile church, like a light shining in the darkness, is a bright witness in a dark world.

Jesus used the metaphor of light in the Sermon on the Mount as a key to understanding the identity and witness of the church: "You are the light of the world. A city set on a hill cannot be hidden. Nor do people light a lamp and put it under a basket, but on a stand, and it gives light to all in the house. In the same way, let your light shine before others, so that they may see your good works and give glory to your Father who is in heaven" (Matt. 5:14–16).

When we put all this together, we can see why the wheat and the weeds are left to grow together—for a time. The church is the light of the world precisely because the one who is himself the light has shined upon us, making us his very children, the children of light among the children of darkness. We all understand the power of light over darkness. The church has been left in the world to shine the transformative light of the gospel into the darkness.

Believers have long struggled with how to understand the role of the church in a fallen world. After all, by God's common grace, there are good aspects to be found even in fallen humanity. But the children of darkness are set against the children of light. Though this conflict may be disguised at various moments in human history, it is always there. James Orr, an evangelical theologian of the late nineteenth century, when describing Christians confronting principalities, powers, ideologies, and worldviews that are in direct conflict with the truth of God's Word, went so far as to say that between the Christian and the secular mind there is always "a deep and radical antagonism."[2]

The greatest theologian of the early church, Augustine, helped Christians to understand our predicament in his great work *De Civitate Dei*, known to us as *The City of God*. Seeking to lead the church even as the Roman Empire was falling, Augustine drew from Scripture in order to remind Christians that we are simultaneously citizens of two different kingdoms—or, to borrow Augustine's terminology, two different cities. We are by birth citizens of the earthly city, but we are by rebirth citizens of the heavenly city. The earthly city and the heavenly city exist together in this age, but the heavenly city is eternal, whereas the earthly city is temporal and temporary. As Augustine understood, Christians often misconstrue this reality. The earthly city looks so powerful, and the church, the visible expression of the heavenly city on earth, can sometimes appear quite powerless. But Augustine thundered with biblical conviction when he made clear that the Christian confidence is that the heavenly city is the focus of God's eternal and omnipotent purposes, whereas the earthly city will pass away under the judgment of God.

Augustine helped the church greatly by considering the question at much greater depth. He confronted the question the disciples had themselves asked. Why is the coming of the kingdom in fullness delayed? Why doesn't Jesus bring the kingdom in its fullness now? Augustine drew faithfully from Scripture in answering the question. The church exists in a fallen age as the children of light in the midst of the children of darkness. We are called to minister faithfully while we await Christ's return, preaching the gospel, demonstrating lives of righteousness and holiness, and loving our neighbors as bearers of the image of God, all to the glory of God. It's tempting to see the earthly city as ultimate, because of its proximity and power. But Christians understand that the earthly city, while worthy of our witness and work, is never worthy of our ultimate allegiance.

If the parable of the weeds is about the church, describing the Christian church as a mixed assembly of weeds and wheat, then the rest of the New Testament becomes unintelligible to us. The church is redefined as nothing more than a microcosm of the world. But Jesus' point in this parable is that the church is actually a microcosm of the kingdom of God, the kingdom of heaven. We should be thankful that Jesus did not leave us in confusion: "The field is the world, and the good seed is the sons of the kingdom" (Matt. 13:38). Thus, the church is in the world as a crop sown by the Lord Jesus Christ himself. In the Lord's fields, the church is called to faithfulness, to witness, to being the torchbearers of the light. The stakes are high, and the distinction between the church and the world is crucial. The church is warned against worldliness, lest the witness of the church be compromised and the light of the gospel be dimmed. By God's grace, we are indeed the children of light in the midst of the children of darkness. But this is all by God's power, and it is his righteousness, not ours, that is revealed in his light.

The parable of the weeds is vital for our understanding of the church's identity and mission in this age of darkness. It also reminds us that even as judgment is coming, it is not the task of the church to bring judgment against the world. The church is to bear witness to the truth through our words and actions, but eternal judgment is in the hands of God alone.

But don't miss the promise for believers. When that awful judgment arrives, bringing "weeping and gnashing of teeth" to the children of darkness, "the righteous will shine like the sun in the kingdom of their Father" (Matt. 13:43), due entirely to God's grace and redeeming love. Could there be a more profound encouragement to the church?

# 4

# And Who Is My Neighbor?

## THE PARABLE OF THE GOOD SAMARITAN

"You have heard that it was said, 'You shall love your neighbor and hate your enemy.' But I say to you, Love your enemies and pray for those who persecute you, so that you may be sons of your Father who is in heaven.... For if you love those who love you, what reward do you have? Do not even tax collectors do the same? And if you greet only your brothers, what more are you doing than others? Do not even the Gentiles do the same?"

—MATTHEW 5:43–47

"You shall love your neighbor as yourself: I am the LORD."

—LEVITICUS 19:18

And a lawyer stood up and put Him to the test, saying, "Teacher, what shall I do to inherit eternal life?" And He said to him, "What is written in the Law? How does it read to you?" And he answered, "YOU SHALL LOVE THE LORD YOUR GOD WITH ALL YOUR HEART, AND WITH ALL YOUR SOUL, AND WITH ALL YOUR STRENGTH, AND WITH ALL YOUR MIND, AND YOUR NEIGHBOR AS YOURSELF." And He said to him, "You have answered correctly; DO THIS, AND YOU WILL LIVE." But wishing to justify himself, he said to Jesus, "And who is my neighbor?"

Jesus replied and said, "A man was going down from Jerusalem to Jericho, and fell among robbers, and they stripped him and beat him, and went away leaving him half dead. And by chance a priest was going down on that road, and when he saw him, he passed by on the other side. Likewise a Levite also, when he came to the place and saw him, passed by on the other side. But a Samaritan, who was on a journey, came upon him; and when he saw him, he felt compassion, and came to him and bandaged up his wounds, pouring oil and wine on them; and he put him on his own beast, and brought him to an inn and took care of him. On the next day he took out two denarii and gave them to the innkeeper and said, 'Take care of him; and whatever more you spend, when I return I will repay you.' Which of these three do you think proved to be a neighbor to the man who fell into the robbers' hands?" And he said, "The one who showed mercy toward him." Then Jesus said to him, "Go and do the same." (Luke 10:25–37 NASB95)

One of the temptations in every age is to reduce the infinitely powerful message of Christ to something more manageable or achievable. We see this happen in many of the precincts of institutional Christianity, where the gospel is supplanted by moralism or replaced with a message of pragmatic self-help. We could frame this temptation as an attempt to domesticate transcendence, reducing the awesome power of the gospel to something a bit tamer.

All of the parables resist that temptation, perhaps none more powerfully than the parable of the good Samaritan. Far more than a memorable story about the importance of treating others with care and respect, this story is about the infinite love of God and the extraordinary expectations God has for his people.

The parable of the good Samaritan (along with the parable of the prodigal son) has become a part of the cultural furniture of the Western world. In one sense, this demonstrates how true it is that Jesus perfected the art of telling parables. But the cultural memory of these parables is a far cry from the parables themselves.

As is so often the case when interpreting a parable, the context is key. Luke 10:25 tells us that a lawyer confronted Jesus in order to "put Him to the test." We see this pattern repeatedly in the New Testament, and it never ends well for the one who challenges Jesus. But we must not rush past the identification of this man. As a lawyer, he was particularly skilled in the Scriptures and in the tradition of Jewish legal reasoning. In the culture of first-century Judaism, learning was highly respected, and the role played by rabbis and teachers of the law was vital. The law was at the center of Judaism as a culture, and those described as lawyers were the greatest scholars of the law, often called upon to render judgments about how the law was to be interpreted and applied in specific, often complicated, situations. Thus, the lawyers were highly admired (although, as depicted in the New Testament, they also had a reputation for complicated reasoning and legalism).

Matthew, Mark, and Luke all reveal encounters between Jesus and those variously described as lawyers, scribes, and Pharisees. In this case, the man who interrogated Jesus was himself a lawyer, a legal and theological authority who appears to have been quite assertive in confronting Jesus and implicitly questioning Jesus' authority as a teacher. The lawyer, intending to put Jesus to the test, posed a crucial question: "Teacher, what shall I do to inherit eternal life?"

The question reveals that this lawyer certainly was not a member of the Sadducees, a group that denied both resurrection and eternal life. Instead, he was asking a question that came down to this: What does God require of us in order that we would be rewarded with everlasting life? Jesus knew that he was talking to a lawyer, and the context of confrontation is clear. Luke explained that the lawyer stood up before speaking to Jesus and addressed him as "teacher," signs of respect for the stature of Jesus in the community and acknowledgment of his role as a teacher with disciples. But despite these signs of respect, the confrontational nature of the question remains clear: this man intended to put Jesus to the test by asking him a deceptively simple question that would lead to complications.

But Jesus turned the tables when he asked the lawyer what the law says. He put the lawyer on the spot, demanding that the lawyer answer his own question. The man responded in a way that would have been shocking to those who heard it, but reflected something Jesus had already said: "You shall love the Lord your God with all your heart, and with all your soul, and with all your strength, and with all your mind; and your neighbor as yourself." Jesus responded to him, "You have answered correctly; do this and you will live."

What was so shocking about the lawyer's answer? It was a surprising combination of two different commands in the Old Testament. The first part would be familiar to every single child of Israel, a famous passage in the Old Testament that was understood to summarize the entire law: "Hear, O Israel: The LORD our God, the LORD is one. You shall love the LORD your God with all your heart and with all your soul and with all your might" (Deut. 6:4–5). That part of the lawyer's response would have been expected and would have reflected the consensus throughout Judaism of the summary of the law. Nevertheless, the man went on to quote, seemingly in a continuous argument, a surprising addition from Leviticus 19:18: "But you shall love your neighbor as yourself."

Christians today take for granted that these two commandments go together. Indeed, Christians commonly refer to these two commandments, put together, as the Great Commandment. What makes the lawyer's response so surprising, and so important, is that he had put together two Old Testament commandments that were not commonly put together in this way. But Christians know that Jesus himself had made clear that the first and greatest commandment is that we are to love the Lord our God with all our heart and soul and mind and that we are also to love our neighbor as ourself.

Speaking of the first commandment, the "Shema," Jesus said, "This is the great and first commandment." But Jesus went on to say that the second "is like it." In other words, Jesus was saying that the first commandment cannot be fulfilled without obedience to the second commandment, love of neighbor. Putting them together, Jesus said, "On these two commandments depend all the Law and the Prophets" (Matt. 22:38–40). Jesus was saying that those two commandments, taken together, are a powerful summary of the entire Law, in one sense, a summary of the entire Old Testament, referred to by Jesus as "the Law and the Prophets." It was Jesus who combined those two commandments, elevating love of neighbor to its status as the necessary demonstration of obedience to the first commandment. Jesus declared that if we do not love our neighbor, we do not truly love God.

So it's no surprise that Jesus told the lawyer, "You have answered correctly; do this and you will live." So far, so good. But, "wishing to justify himself," the lawyer pressed the confrontation further and posed another question to Jesus: "And who is my neighbor?"

We must not miss the arrogance of the lawyer's question. It was not just a simple request for Jesus to define who was (and, presumably, who was not) his neighbor. The lawyer was insinuating that there were some who simply were not worthy to be considered his neighbor. His obedience to Leviticus 19:18, and thus to the entire law, only extended to those he considered worthy of neighbor status.

This context of confrontation—and the lawyer's arrogant desire to define and restrict the scope of the category of neighbor—is vital for understanding the parable of the good Samaritan. In its structure and detail, the story is something that Jesus' hearers would have immediately understood. He referred to real places and to a familiar threat. When Jesus spoke of a man who was going down from Jerusalem to Jericho, the listeners would have immediately been able to picture the steep wilderness path from Jerusalem (located about 2,500 feet above sea level) to Jericho (800 feet below sea level). That road was infamously dangerous, the scene of frequent robberies. So Jesus' audience would not have been surprised that the man in the story, who is never identified in terms of his ethnicity or religion, fell among robbers who assaulted him, stripped him of his clothes and possessions, and left him to die. Jesus described him as "half dead."

But then Jesus moved on from this easy-to-imagine scenario to describe a progression of passersby. The first was a priest who, when he saw the half-dead man, "passed by on the other side"—a picture of unconscionable neglect and lack of care. Jesus' spare use of words leaves us to imagine this callous priest hugging the other side of the road, not even coming close enough to the man to verify whether he was dead or alive. Being a priest, he was likely concerned about ritual cleanness. Coming into contact with a dead person would have rendered him unable to fulfill his priestly responsibilities until he had met the requirements of the law for cleansing.

All of that, of course, is in the background, but the brutal fact is that this priest passed the man by as if he were not worthy of attention. He saw no urgency, because he saw no neighbor worthy of the love God had commanded. Implicit in this context is that the priest may very well have considered himself to be beyond obligation to this man because he did not consider the man his neighbor. In the context of the lawyer's confrontational question to Jesus, the fact that the first passerby is a priest strikes a blow to the very heart of a self-righteous, legalistic strand of first-century Judaism.

The second passerby was a Levite, a member of the lower priestly order responsible for serving the priesthood. The Levite behaved just like the priest, passing the man "on the other side." Neither bothered to cross the road to see if the man might be saved. The stage was now set for a third character who would happen upon the man, and his example would stand in stark contrast to the priest and the Levite. The third character was simply identified as a Samaritan.

It is difficult for modern readers to understand how disconcerting Jesus' story would have been to his hearers. Jesus could have chosen any number of characters for this third example, but he chose a Samaritan. Jesus chose an ethnic and religious identity for this man that was clearly calculated to explode his audience's concept of neighbor.

It is tempting for contemporary readers to think of a Samaritan merely as someone from outside the Jewish community. But for Jewish people at that time, Samaritans were something much worse than mere outsiders. Centuries before, the people known in the first century as Samaritans had violated the Jewish law, disobeyed God, and compromised with conquering and neighboring peoples by abandoning scriptural obedience and by intermarrying with people from outside of Israel. The Samaritans practiced what amounted to a new religion, a perversion of Judaism. Furthermore, the Samaritans rejected the Jews' claim that Jerusalem was the proper center of worship and had even desecrated the Jewish temple some years before Jesus told this parable, deliberately rendering the temple unusable for sacrifice during the holy days.

In short, Jews in Jesus' day despised the Samaritans for their idolatry and for their lawbreaking. Jesus could not have chosen a more controversial identity for this parable's protagonist.

When the Samaritan saw the half-dead man, "he felt compassion." That's the crucial shift in the parable. All the Samaritan's subsequent acts of kindness grew from that initial moment of experiencing compassion for a fellow human being. Jesus' message is clear: we are to have compassion for all people, regardless of circumstance, ethnicity, beliefs, or perceived acceptability.

The Samaritan's compassion was then channeled into practical care. He went to the half-dead man, touched him, bandaged up his wounds, anointed him with oil and wine, then set him on his own pack animal and brought him to an inn so that he would receive care. The Samaritan had already demonstrated his generosity by using the precious substances of oil and wine to cleanse the man's wounds. Now, after bringing the half-dead man to the inn, he paid the innkeeper in advance to ensure that the man would be cared for, promising that upon his return he would repay any further costs that may have been incurred.

The Samaritan demonstrated compassion that went well beyond expectations. Though Samaritans and Jews were bitter enemies, he provided costly and practical care, treating the half-dead man as if he were a member of his own family. The picture of the Samaritan's compassion remains with us and has spread throughout our cultural imagination, simply because of the story's graphic power and the moral urgency of its message.

But remember that Jesus told this parable in answer to a lawyer's question and in the context of confrontation. The lawyer who sought to justify himself had demanded that Jesus answer his question, "And who is my neighbor?" The crucial issue there is the pronoun. The man was demanding that Jesus offer a specific limitation to who qualified as *my* neighbor. But after telling the story of the compassionate Samaritan, Jesus turned the question back upon the lawyer.

"Which of these three do you think proved to be a neighbor to the man who fell into the robbers' hands?" Jesus asked. The question was presented brilliantly. Jesus asked the man for his own opinion, as a lawyer, as to who proved to be a neighbor. Jesus also ensured that the issue here was not theoretical but deeply theological and practical. It's one thing to agree in theory that someone is our neighbor. It is an entirely different thing to be moved by compassion and then to *prove* to be a neighbor.

The lawyer's answer was simple: "The one who showed mercy toward him." This was the only answer he could possibly have given. The man sought to entrap Jesus in a question, but, as was so often the case, Jesus turned the question upon his accuser. The man was seeking to subvert the teaching authority of Jesus, but he ended up being trapped in a question of his own arrogant devising. After Jesus told the parable, contrasting the complete failure of the priest and the Levite with the faithfulness of the Samaritan, the lawyer had no choice but to agree that the neighbor was "the one who showed mercy toward him." Don't pass too quickly by the fact that the man answered by specifically mentioning that the Samaritan "showed mercy toward him."

We sometimes use the word *mercy* in a sloppy and unthinking way, reducing it to being merely a synonym for *kindness*. But the Bible reveals that mercy is a costly type of love, compassion that is willing to pay a price. Mercy is what a court might extend to a criminal, what a king might extend to a subject, what God in Christ extends to sinners. This Samaritan proved himself to be the neighbor of the half-dead man by showing him mercy. Jesus then told the lawyer, "Go and do the same."

The power of this parable is as gripping in our generation as it was when Jesus first spoke it to this lawyer and those who overheard the conversation. It is one of Jesus' most famous parables in the popular imagination precisely because of the graphic nature of the parable and its moral impact. But here is where we have to understand that the parable is so much more than an inspiring story about someone who went beyond the call of duty in exercising compassion. Jesus was making a comprehensive theological point: we are to consider all human beings as our neighbor. There is not a single human being, made in God's image, who does not deserve our compassion, care, and mercy. The example of the Samaritan grabs our attention and renders us powerless to come up with any exception to who deserves our mercy.

Even in this fallen world we see examples of God's common grace at work, built into human nature and the created order. People feel compassion and act with generosity and care toward those who suffer. We must certainly affirm the moral truth in this parable that every single human being is to treat every other human being as a neighbor. But take care not to reduce the parable just to this moral message. Beyond such general lessons about neighborly care, Scripture constrains Christians to understand that we owe something to every single fellow image-bearer of God. Karl Marx reportedly loved humanity but hated human beings. This must not be true of Jesus' disciples. The biblical worldview begins with the fundamental truth that all human beings are made in God's image. This transcends all earthly markers of human identity, from ethnicity and race to kinship and people, language and culture. We are called to love both humanity *and* the individual human beings who comprise that humanity.

The parable also reveals that proximity matters. The priest and the Levite are not judged because they failed someone far beyond the reach of their care. They failed someone right in front of them. The biblical principle of subsidiarity affirms that our care is most urgently needed by those right before us. The judgment against the priest and the Levite is that they did not even cross the road to help a man right before their eyes. There is a sense in which we owe our care to every single human being in the world. But there is a greater sense in which we owe care most specifically to those we can immediately care for and tend to.

What exactly do Christians owe all human beings as our neighbors? This parable does not suggest that Christianity should be understood simply as one giant ministry of practical philanthropy. The establishment of so many hospitals and orphanages and care ministries throughout the history of the Christian church is indeed a testimony to the compassion of Christ's people. But all those ministries grow out of a deeper, more urgent compassion.

Christians owe to all people our witness to the gospel of Jesus Christ. Jesus himself made this clear not only in the Great Commission but in his constant sending of disciples into the world with the gospel. We owe to all persons the good news of salvation through faith in Jesus Christ. We also owe to all people our prayers for their cares and concerns. This is certainly included in the Lord's Prayer, where Jesus told his disciples to pray to our heavenly Father that his will would be done "on earth as it is in heaven" (Matt. 6:10). That points the church not only to prayer but to action. Christians are called to specific acts of care and concern, recognizing that there is no theological, political, ideological, or cultural boundary limiting who is our neighbor.

That there is no boundary when it comes to identifying our neighbor would have been the most astounding part of Jesus' message to those who heard it first. In truth, it is equally astounding now. As we saw in the parable of the weeds, Jesus made a clear distinction between the church and the world, but he also drove home the reality that the church is in the world to serve as his people in work and in witness. The parable of the good Samaritan helps us understand how that is to be done.

But as we think about the parable of the good Samaritan, we need to consider anew how the parable is fixed in our memory. For one thing, Jesus did not refer to the Samaritan as "good." He simply identified him as a Samaritan. His acts were genuinely good and compassionate and merciful. But the Samaritan is never described as good. In the truest sense, only one human being deserves to be called good, and that is Jesus Christ, truly God and truly man. The one who spoke this parable is the one who is our ultimate Rescuer, Redeemer, and Savior. Jesus himself told us, "Greater love has no one than this, that someone lay down his life for his friends" (John 15:13).

The message of the Samaritan's compassion is all the more powerful when we consider who spoke the parable. Jesus was headed for the cross, the ultimate example of refusing to pass by on the other side and choosing instead to show mercy at great personal cost. John 3:16 reveals God's unbounded, costly compassion in just a few beautiful words: "For God so loved the world, that he gave his only Son, that whoever believes in him should not perish but have eternal life." The apostle John shared that Christlike love should be the mark of every Christian: "By this we know love, that he laid down his life for us, and we ought to lay down our lives for the brothers" (1 John 3:16).

Jesus had compassion for us, crossed the road, and went to Calvary. And thus, we are saved.

# 5

# Even If One Should Rise from the Dead

## THE PARABLE OF THE RICH MAN AND LAZARUS

For the Word of God is living and active, sharper than any two-edged sword, piercing to the division of soul and of spirit, of joints and of marrow, and discerning the thoughts and intentions of the heart.

—HEBREWS 4:12

The grass withers, the flower fades, but the word of our God will stand forever.

—ISAIAH 40:8

But as for you, continue in what you have learned and have firmly believed, knowing from whom you learned it and how from childhood you have been acquainted with the sacred writings, which are able to make you wise for salvation through faith in Christ Jesus. All Scripture is breathed out by God and profitable for teaching, for reproof, for correction, and for training in righteousness, that the man of God may be complete, equipped for every good work.

—2 TIMOTHY 3:14–17

"Now there was a rich man, and he habitually dressed in purple and fine linen, joyously living in splendor every day. And a poor man named Lazarus was laid at his gate, covered with sores, and longing to be fed with the crumbs which were falling from the rich man's table; besides, even the dogs were coming and licking his sores. Now the poor man died and was carried away by the angels to Abraham's bosom; and the rich man also died and was buried. In Hades, he lifted up his eyes, being in torment, and saw Abraham far away and Lazarus in his bosom. And he cried out and said, 'Father Abraham, have mercy on me, and send Lazarus so that he may dip the tip of his finger in water and cool off my tongue, for I am in agony in this flame.' But Abraham said, 'Child, remember that during your life you received your good things, and likewise Lazarus bad things; but now he is being comforted here, and you are in agony. And besides all this, between us and you there is a great chasm fixed, so that those who wish to come over here to you will not be able, and that none may cross over from there to us.' And he said, 'Then I beg you, father, that you send him to my father's house—for I have five brothers—in order that he may warn them, so that they will not also come to this place of torment.' But Abraham said, 'They have Moses and the Prophets; let them hear them.' But he said, 'No, father Abraham, but if someone goes to them from the dead, they will repent!' But he said to him, 'If they do not listen to Moses and the Prophets, they will not be persuaded even if someone rises from the dead.'" (Luke 16:19–31 NASB95)

Back in 1985, theologian J. I. Packer spoke about what he called the "Thirty Years' War" over the Bible (1955–1985). During those decades, some of the most important debates about the nature and authority of Scripture took place, particularly in regard to the absolute truthfulness and inerrancy of the Bible. There can be no doubt that those decades were crucial, with faithful theologians battling the long effort in the modern age to deny the inspiration and authority of the Bible as God's Word. But there has been a war over the inspiration and authority of God's Word since Genesis 3, when Satan sought to subvert God's word in the garden.

Christians must affirm all the perfections of God's Word. We begin with Scripture's own testimony to its divine authorship, which drives us to affirm what is known as the "plenary verbal doctrine of inspiration": God is the ultimate Author of Scripture, and the Holy Spirit has inspired every single word of it. The other perfections of Scripture include its clarity, its authority, its infallibility, its trustworthiness, its unity, and its sufficiency. That last perfection of God's Word—its sufficiency—is one of the most neglected affirmations of Scripture found within the Bible itself.

Jesus' parables often end up surprising us by the conclusion of the story, sometimes catching us completely off guard. That is the case with the parable of the rich man and Lazarus found in Luke 16:19–31. This passage appears at first to be about God's judgment upon the self-sufficient rich, but it then turns into a crucial affirmation of the reality of eternal judgment and the justice of God in hell. But then, at the end, it turns out that the main purpose behind the parable is Jesus' revelation of the sufficiency of God's Word.

There are some who question whether this passage is indeed a parable. It follows a parabolic structure, beginning with the simple statement, introducing characters, and proceeding with a basic story. Yet some interpreters point out that parables are stories, not statements of propositional truth—and within the passage is a clear propositional teaching about hell. But this should not surprise us at all, for almost all the parables include some propositional truth, and every one of the parables, without exception, points to the objective truth of the gospel and the kingdom of God. There should be no question at all that when Jesus spoke of hell in this passage, he intended his audience, as well as us, to take his description of hell as literal truth, which it surely is. The text is best understood as a parable that conveys propositional truth. There is no indeterminacy of meaning here. To the contrary, the meaning of the parable is profoundly clear.

Jesus began by describing a rich man who was so wealthy that he dressed every day in purple and linen and treated every day as a festival or feast day. You might think that this is an exaggerated character, but it is actually a depiction of the nouveau riche of the Roman Empire in the first century. As in so many cultures, there were class distinctions. At the top was the imperial power, but then there were successive rings of power, each with symbols and accoutrements of status. There was also an explosion of wealth among the aristocracy in Rome, and those who were avid social climbers sought to imitate the increasingly ostentatious displays of wealth in Rome. The truth is that Rome was not unique in this pattern. Virtually every society shows the distinctions between those who are the haves and those who are the have-nots. In between are those who want to look as if they hold a higher status than they can afford. The exaggerated display of wealth that describes the rich man in this passage is just a display of that kind of social climbing, a desperate demonstration of status. Purple was a rare and costly dye color, and linen was a particularly expensive cloth, so to dress in purple linen every day was an unmistakable (if tasteless) advertisement of one's wealth. This man's ostentatiousness extended beyond his dress to his diet. We are told that he feasted sumptuously every day. Later we read that the second character in the parable, Lazarus, could have survived by eating "the crumbs which were falling from the rich man's table." This is a man who had a terminal case of conspicuous consumption and moral indifference.

The rich man's wealth was not the issue. Rather, it was his trust in riches and how he had tied his personal security, hope, and identity to his material wealth. In Proverbs 11:28 we read, "Whoever trusts in his riches will fall, but the righteous will flourish like a green leaf." One of the seductive aspects of being wealthy is finding security in that wealth. But the notion of human self-sufficiency is antithetical to saving faith. This myth of self-sufficiency turns out to be fatal, with eternal consequences. Writing to Christians, Paul spoke of those who are "rich in this present age," telling Timothy to "charge them not to be haughty, not to set their hopes on the uncertainty of riches, but on God, who richly provides us with everything to enjoy" (1 Tim. 6:17). That clear warning flies in the face of the prosperity theology that has infected so much of American religion and has been exported abroad.

Prosperity theology is a refutation of the gospel of Jesus Christ. It tells us that we are to expect riches by the exercise of faith and that we are to find security in those riches. Prosperity theology is heresy not because it promises too much, but because it promises too little. The health and wealth that prosperity preachers promise their followers are temporary. Furthermore, it turns out that those who follow the prosperity preachers rarely become rich, even if the preachers do.

The gospel of Jesus Christ doesn't promise less than prosperity theology. It promises infinitely more. In Christ we are assured of salvation from sin, of the gift of everlasting life, and of the joy of being united with him forever. We are told that we are citizens of a heavenly kingdom and that, like Lazarus, we will be honored in paradise as those who are Christ's own.

The second character is, of course, Lazarus, described as a poor man who was covered with sores and laid at the man's gate. The presence of the gate indicates just how wealthy the rich man was. It would not have been uncommon for someone in great need to be laid at the gates of a rich man in order to perhaps spark the rich man's philanthropy and care. Nevertheless, this rich man was clearly unmoved and he allowed a poor man laid at his gate to grow weaker and weaker, despite knowing that the man could have survived on the crumbs from his table.

That Lazarus was covered with sores would, according to some of the conventional wisdom of the day, indicate that he was cursed by God. You'll recall the same picture from the Old Testament book of Job. The added detail that "even the dogs were coming and licking his sores" completes the picture of Lazarus's utter degradation. The dogs referred to in Scripture were not canine companions. They were scavengers who were not only competing with Lazarus for food, but likely saw Lazarus *as* food.

The first great surprise of the parable emerges when the poor man died and was "carried away by the angels to Abraham's bosom." According to the conventional thinking of the period, Lazarus's suffering and poverty would indicate that he was cursed by God and headed toward a judgment that would place him outside of divine honor. But, to the contrary, when the poor man died he was not only received by God but also was accompanied by an angelic honor guard and placed at the side of Abraham—the position of greatest honor in the Jewish imagination, since Abraham is the paradigm of faith, the father of the Jewish people, the one with whom God made his covenant and through whom all the peoples of the earth will be blessed.

This parable would have been jarring, and perhaps even offensive, to those hearing it. How in the world could poor Lazarus, who had died in indignity and had his sores licked by dogs, be honored at Abraham's side?

But Jesus did not give his audience long to consider that question because he went immediately to the fact that the rich man also died—and was sent to hades, the realm of the dead, where he was in torment.

We have here the conjunction of two great themes of Scripture. The first is the "great reversal" in which we find that what passes for power and dignity and success in one life may lead to a very different result in the life to come. The great reversal may be between the rich and the poor, or it may be between the powerful and the powerless. But there can be no doubt that much of the prophetic teaching of the Old Testament pointed out that "the powers that be" and the disadvantaged on earth will undergo a reversal in heaven, on the other side of God's judgment.

But the great reversal is joined by this affirmation of the coming judgment resulting in two destinies, salvation and damnation. Here we have a direct contrast between the objective realities of heaven and of hell. The solace and joy and comfort of heaven is contrasted with the torments of hell. The language here is simple and straightforward, clear and nonevasive. The rich man was in physical torment. We know this because he cried out to father Abraham that Lazarus would come and dip the end of his finger in water and cool the rich man's tongue, "for I am in agony in this flame." In this parable, the reality of judgment resulting in the dual destinies of salvation and damnation is unavoidable and clear. It is not just a part of the narrative revealed in this parable; it is a biblical truth that Jesus referred to in several parables, where he spoke of the judgment to come and warned of a place of "weeping and gnashing of teeth."

The Bible is straightforward and clear about the inevitability of God's coming judgment. It will be absolutely just, even as God himself is just, and it will be the final judgment in which all secrets will be revealed and all sin will be judged. The message of the gospel tells us that the only escape from the torments of hell, understood clearly as the just judgment of God upon human sinfulness, is the salvation that comes only through faith in the Lord Jesus Christ and our repentance from sin. Jesus underlined the reality and horror of hell repeatedly, and this parable is no exception.

Hell is a controversial issue in our times. Even in Jesus' day there were those who rejected the idea of the afterlife and everlasting punishment, such as the Sadducees. But there can be no question that the Bible sets out the reality of hell and the righteousness of God's judgment in stark terms. With the coming of the modern age, the doctrine of hell became an embarrassment to those who wanted a Christianity that was culturally sophisticated and inoffensive. Let's be clear—there is no doctrine more offensive to human pride than the reality of hell. One of the first signs of the rapid development of liberal theology in Europe and throughout the English-speaking world was the attempt to subvert the doctrine of hell. By the time we reached the second half of the twentieth century, theological liberalism had infected many denominations, and the denial of hell had become commonplace. For many people in today's postmodern world, the biblical doctrine of hell has become simply unthinkable.

During the Enlightenment, the father of theological liberalism, Friedrich Schleiermacher, sought to make Christianity relevant and palatable to the "cultured despisers" of religion. But in order to do this, Schleiermacher and theologians inspired by his approach had to throw the doctrine of hell overboard. If they did not deny the doctrine entirely, they sought to redefine it in a way that would be less offensive to modern sensibilities. In the words of one observer, they sought to "air-condition hell."[1]

The first step toward redefining hell was the denial of the clear teachings of Scripture about hell as a place of everlasting torment followed by the suggestion that hell might be a place where moral reform would be produced. This coincided with vast changes in Western civilization's understanding of the nature of crime and punishment. The second step was to reconceptualize God himself as love without justice, benevolence without wrath. Selecting some attributes of God at the expense of others is exactly what faithful Christians must not do. We must always remember that God has revealed himself to us in Scripture as infinite in all of his perfections. We can never set his holiness over against his love, his mercy over against his justice. Instead, we must receive all that is revealed about God in Scripture.

The faithful conception of righteousness is based on the infinite righteousness of God himself—a perfect righteousness. Christ alone fulfills the Father's righteousness, and he did so objectively—revealing an objectively *true* righteousness. By the power of the gospel, Christ's righteousness is imputed to believers. The difference between heaven and hell is the presence or absence of that *objectively real* righteousness.

Later theologians, including liberal theologians of the nineteenth and twentieth centuries, denied the importance of that objective righteousness and adopted something like a sliding scale of human righteousness. Salvation itself became more subjective, based in experience, and less objective—there was no need for the atonement of Christ. Hell was redefined to match the new theology.

Some theologians have even suggested that the doctrine of hell is immoral, asserting that a place of eternal torment doesn't seem compatible with a loving God. Here we have a classic case of human morality standing in judgment of divine reality. It is difficult to imagine a more profound inversion of the truth. We will not be judging God. God will be judging us, perfectly and justly in accordance with his own character. Rejecting God's self-revelation in favor of our own ideas about what he would or wouldn't do is the height of self-righteous pride.

Returning to our overview of the parable, Jesus explained that the rich man, seeing Lazarus comforted at Abraham's side in paradise, begged, "Father Abraham, have mercy on me, and send Lazarus so that he may dip the tip of his finger in water and cool off my tongue, for I am in agony in this flame." Abraham replied, "Child, remember that during your life you received your good things, and likewise Lazarus bad things; but now he is being comforted here, and you are in agony." Then Abraham told the rich man, "Between us and you there is a great chasm fixed, so that those who wish to come over from here to you will not be able, and that none may cross over from there to us."

In this parable we hear the closing of a door for eternity. On the other side of divine judgment there is no appeal, no rescue. As noted earlier, this parable is telling us literal truths about the kingdom, even as it catches us by surprise with the flow of the narrative. We can imagine the rich man in torment in the realm of the dead and Lazarus being comforted. We can sense the rich man's unspeakable pain. But then we hear the finality of Abraham's verdict. *No one can go from hades to paradise, nor from paradise to hades.*

Now the parable takes its most unexpected and remarkable turn. The rich man issued a new request, asking Abraham to send Lazarus to his father's house to warn and call to repentance his five brothers who were still alive, "so that they will not also come to this place of torment." We now learn that the issue at stake is not merely God's judgment upon the rich man's claims of self-sufficiency or the objective reality of heaven, hell, and divine judgment. The core message is the sufficiency of Scripture. Through the voice of Abraham, Jesus explained that the rich man's brothers already had a witness sufficient to call them to repentance: Holy Scripture. "They have Moses and the Prophets; let them hear them." The phrase "Moses and the Prophets" was a common way of referring to the Law and the Prophets, that is, the Hebrew Scriptures, which Christians call the Old Testament.

The rich man, arguing that the Scripture is not enough, made a final desperate bid: "But if someone goes to them from the dead, they will repent!" Here the parable reaches its climax. Speaking again through Abraham, Jesus said, "If they do not listen to Moses and the Prophets, they will not be persuaded even if someone rises from the dead."

Here we see the astounding verdict of Jesus—the one who would soon rise from the dead himself. Jesus knew what lay ahead: his crucifixion, burial, and resurrection. He knew that those who had denied him prior to his resurrection would for the most part continue to deny him after God raised him from the dead. Through Abraham Jesus made clear in this parable that the issue for the church in every age is whether we really believe in the sufficiency of Scripture. Sinners must hear the call of the gospel in order to believe and be saved. What evidence do we bring to them? What case do we make for belief in the Lord Jesus Christ? The truth is that we have nothing beyond the Scriptures. We must affirm emphatically that Scripture is sufficient to reveal everything needful for our salvation, for the Christian life, for the establishment of right doctrine, for the conducting of right worship, and for answering questions about how Christians are to live faithfully in the world. We must not look for any subsequent revelation or extrabiblical information to guide us to eternal truth and a life of Christian faithfulness.

Furthermore, we have no means of reaching the lost other than sharing the gospel and preaching the Word of God. As Martin Luther affirmed, the right preaching of the Word of God is the first and most essential mark of the Christian church. God does his saving work through the preaching of the Word of God. The Holy Spirit opens hearts to believe by the preaching of the Word of God. Sinners are convinced of the truth concerning Christ and of the reality of their own sin by the ministry of the Holy Spirit through the preaching of the Word of God. The church is matured into the likeness of Christ by the preaching of the Word of God.

In short, we live by the Word of God.

Sadly, many people familiar with the parable of the rich man and Lazarus have no idea of its central message. In a strange sense, this goes back again to the necessity of our trust in the sufficiency of Scripture. We have to turn to Scripture as the inspired and inerrant and sufficient Word of God and live as the people of the Word, under the authority of the Word, looking to the Word of God as God's gift to us, whereby he reveals all things necessary for our salvation and faithfulness.

One of the great documents of the Christian tradition, the Westminster Confession of Faith, affirms the sufficiency of Scripture with these words: "The whole counsel of God concerning all things necessary for His own glory, man's salvation, faith in life, is either expressly set down in Scripture, or by good and necessary consequence may be deduced from Scripture; unto which nothing at any time is to be added, whether by new revelations of the Spirit, or traditions of men."

The great emphatic point of this parable is that those who will not hear the Scripture will not hear anything or anyone else. They will not repent, even if they are confronted with one who has risen from the dead. The one who *did* rise from the dead told us this on his own divine authority.

# 6

# Redemption, Rejoicing, and Rejection in Luke 15

## THE PARABLES OF THE LOST LAMB, THE LOST COIN, AND THE LOST SONS

All we like sheep have gone astray; we have turned— every one—to his own way; and the Lord has laid on him the iniquity of us all.

—ISAIAH 53:6

"I will seek the lost, and I will bring back the strayed, and I will bind up the injured, and I will strengthen the weak."

—EZEKIEL 34:16

"All that the Father gives me will come to me, and whoever comes to me I will never cast out. For I have come down from heaven, not to do my own will but the will of him who sent me. And this is the will of him who sent me, that I should lose nothing of all he has given me, but raise it up on the last day."

—JOHN 6:37–39

Now all the tax collectors and the sinners were coming near Him to listen to Him. Both the Pharisees and the scribes began to grumble, saying, "This man receives sinners and eats with them."

So He told them this parable, saying, "What man among you, if he has a hundred sheep and has lost one of them, does not leave the ninety-nine in the open pasture and go after the one which is lost until he finds it? When he has found it, he lays it on his shoulders, rejoicing. And when he comes home, he calls together his friends and his neighbors, saying to them, 'Rejoice with me, for I have found my sheep which was lost.' I tell you that in the same way, there will be more joy in heaven over one sinner who repents than over ninety-nine righteous persons who need no repentance.

"Or what woman, if she has ten silver coins and loses one coin, does not light a lamp and sweep the house and search carefully until she finds it? When she has found it, she calls together her friends and neighbors, saying, 'Rejoice with me, for I have found the coin which I had lost!' In the same way, I tell you, there is joy in the presence of the angels of God over one sinner who repents."

And He said, "A man had two sons. The younger of them said to his father, 'Father, give me the share of the estate that falls to me.' So he divided his wealth between them. And not many days later, the younger son gathered everything together and went on a journey into a distant country, and there he squandered his estate with loose living. Now when he had spent everything, a severe famine occurred in that country, and he began to be impoverished. So he went and hired himself out to one of the citizens of that country, and he sent him into his fields to feed swine. And he would have gladly filled his stomach with the pods that the swine were eating, and no one was giving anything to him.

"But when he came to his senses, he said, 'How many of my father's hired men have more than enough bread, but I am dying here with hunger! I will get up and go to my father, and will say to him, "Father, I have sinned against heaven, and in your sight; I am no longer worthy to be called your son; make me as one of your hired men."' So he got up and came to his father. But while he was still a long way off, his father saw him and felt compassion for him, and ran and embraced him and kissed him. And the son said to him, 'Father, I have sinned against heaven and in your sight. I am no longer worthy to be called your son.' But the father said to his slaves, 'Quickly bring out the best robe and put it on him, and put a ring on his hand and sandals on his feet; and bring the fattened calf, kill it, and let us eat and celebrate; for this son of mine was dead and has come to life again; he was lost and has been found.' And they began to celebrate.

"Now his older son was in the field, and when he came and approached the house, he heard music and dancing. And he summoned one of the servants and began inquiring what these things could be. And he said to him, 'Your brother has come, and your father has killed the fattened calf because he has received him back safe and sound.' But he became angry and was not willing to go in; and his father came out and began pleading with him. But he answered and said to his father, 'Look! For so many years I have been serving you and I have never neglected a command of yours; and yet you have never given me a young goat, so that I might celebrate with my friends; but when this son of yours came, who has devoured your wealth with prostitutes, you killed the fattened calf for him.' And he said to him, 'Son, you have always been with me, and all that is mine is yours. But we had to celebrate and rejoice, for this brother of yours was dead and has begun to live, and was lost and has been found.'" (Luke 15 NASB95)

We learn early in life that there are few experiences more frustrating than losing something, and there are few experiences so frightening as being lost.

When I was a boy, I was fascinated with the black-and-white television series *Lost in Space*. The idea was that a space exploration mission had gone awry, and a small group of humans (including a young boy about the age I was at the time) was lost in outer space with little hope of finding their way back home. The show's tone was comedic, but watching it as a young boy, I still sensed the fear and horror that would surely accompany the realization that one is truly, permanently lost.

In Luke 15 we encounter a cycle of three parables about lostness. Though each story depicts the experience of losing something precious, they are actually about the universal human experience of *being* lost—separated from God and alienated from our Creator. That is the spiritual state of all humans apart from Christ—and it is that very lostness (or the denial of that lostness) that makes the parables in

Luke 15 so unspeakably powerful. These three parables of lostness all follow the same narrative pattern, with a dramatic surprise at the end.

When Jesus told these parables, tax collectors and sinners had gathered in order to hear him speak and teach. But Luke notes that there were also Pharisees and scribes present, and they were grumbling. Their grumbling was not initially about what Jesus was saying, but about the fact that he was overly friendly with tax collectors and other notorious sinners—allowing them to follow him around and even sharing meals with them.

The conventional theology of the Pharisees and the scribes led them to keep as much distance as possible between themselves and anyone known to be involved in sin. Proximity was a theological issue to these legalists: they made every effort to maintain clear separation between themselves and those they considered to be sinners, bolstering their own sense of self-righteousness.

There is also no doubt that the tax collectors and sinners who were coming to Jesus were notorious. To say "tax collector" in Judea in the first century was to say "thief." Tax collectors colluded with Rome. Operating something like local franchisees, tax collectors set up their own business, inflating the tax rate and skimming the extra proceeds as their own income. They made themselves rich while making the people poor. In short, tax collectors were universally despised in first-century Judea—making the salvation of a tax collector a remarkable picture of God's grace! It sent a powerful signal in the first century that continues today: God's grace can reach even the greatest of sinners.

The other sinners identified in Luke's introduction to the chapter are those whose sinful lifestyles were so notorious that they were generally ostracized. Most rabbis would have followed the conventional wisdom of the day and kept their distance from any sinners. Further, showing hospitality was considered a way of extending respect to individuals or groups. For Jesus to extend a table fellowship to tax collectors and sinners was to indicate that he considered them within the bounds of human society.

This is not to suggest that Jesus was endorsing or overlooking their sin. The Gospels make clear that Jesus condemned sin in every form, regardless of context. But Jesus had come to preach salvation to those who needed it—and making that point was exactly Jesus' purpose in this cycle of parables.

In Luke 5, Jesus saw the tax collector named Levi (Matthew), sitting at his tax booth, and simply said to him, "Follow me." Levi immediately rose and followed Jesus. Crucially, Levi left everything behind, including his income by tax collection and his status as a tax collector. By simple obedience to the call of Jesus, he was transformed into one of Jesus' disciples. In the same passage, we are told that Levi made a great feast for Jesus in his house and the guests included "a large company of tax collectors and others reclining at table with them."

Predictably, the Pharisees and the scribes grumbled about this, asking, "Why do you eat and drink with tax collectors and sinners?" Jesus famously answered the Pharisees, "Those who are well have no need of a physician, but those who are sick. I have not come to call the righteous but sinners to repentance" (vv. 27–32). Keep those words in mind as you consider the grumbling that took place as Jesus told this cycle of three parables. Some in his audience knew they were lost, but he was simultaneously telling these parables to those who believed themselves to be anything but lost.

The first parable had to do with a lost lamb. Jesus asked an interesting question: "What man among you, if he has a hundred sheep and has lost one of them, does not leave the ninety-nine in the open pasture and go after the one which is lost until he finds it?" Now, the blunt fact is that no sane shepherd would leave ninety-nine sheep alone in the open country in order to go after one lost lamb. Any shepherd who opted to leave ninety-nine to go after one would end up with a hundred lost sheep.

But that is the point, as Jesus was setting up an exaggerated situation to show us the infinite nature of God's love for sinners—like a shepherd who will not rest until he finds the lost lamb, carries it home on his shoulders, and celebrates with joy. In fact, the shepherd's joy is contagious. He calls together his friends to celebrate with him: "Rejoice with me, for I have found my sheep which was lost!"

But then Jesus took his audience from this earthly picture to the heavenly reality: "I tell you that in the same way, there will be more joy in heaven over one sinner who repents than over ninety-nine righteous persons who need no repentance." Note carefully that Jesus was not saying that some people, on the basis of their own righteousness, will be acceptable to God on the Day of Judgment. The Bible is extremely clear that there is no one righteous in that sense. Paul described salvation as gaining Christ and being found in him: "Not having a righteousness of my own that comes from the law, but that which comes through faith in Christ, the righteousness from God that depends on faith" (Phil. 3:9). Romans 3:10 simply claims that there is no one righteous, "no, not one," echoing the clear message of the Old Testament. Twice in the Psalms (Ps. 14:3; 53:3) we are told "there is none who does good, not even one." And in Ecclesiastes 7:20, we are reminded, "Surely there is not a righteous man on earth who does good and never sins." Thus, Jesus was saying that what causes joy to break out in heaven is when one lost sheep is found, when one sinner comes home and repents.

The Old Testament also describes the redeeming love of God as a shepherd finding sheep. Isaiah 53:6 says, "All we like sheep have gone astray; we have turned—every one—to his own way; and the LORD has laid on him the iniquity of us all." When we hear Jesus speak of his mission to "the lost sheep of the house of Israel" (Matt. 15:24), we're reminded of the prophet Jeremiah speaking of the people who "have been lost sheep" (Jer. 50:6).

There is also an Old Testament dimension to our understanding of the shepherd's absolute determination to find this one lost sheep. In Ecclesiastes 3:6, we are reminded of the cycle of times. There is "a time to search and a time to give up as lost" (NASB95). But this is precisely what God does not do. In his sovereign determination to save sinners, God does not give sinners up as lost. The shepherd in this parable becomes a picture of God's redeeming love. Once the sheep is found, that love turns into rejoicing, for the sheep was lost and now is found. Rejoicing breaks out among the shepherd's friends, but also in the precincts of heaven.

And in Psalm 23, we find David's beautiful picture of God as his shepherd:

> The LORD is my shepherd; I shall not want. He makes me lie down in green pastures. He leads me beside still waters. He restores my soul. He leads me in paths of righteousness for his name's sake. Even though I walk through the valley of the shadow of death, I will fear no evil, for you are with me; your rod and your staff, they comfort me. You prepare a table before me in the presence of my enemies; you anoint my head with oil; my cup overflows. Surely goodness and mercy shall follow me all the days of my life, and I shall dwell in the house of the LORD forever.

These words are so precious to believers precisely because we know ourselves to be sheep who survive only by the love and care of our shepherd. God's love toward his own, as described in this remarkable psalm, set the religion of Israel over against all idolatries. God is not the impassive creator of the cosmos who has left us alone and lost, nor is he a petty, vengeful tyrant. To the contrary, he is a loving Shepherd who guides and nourishes our souls, leading us in paths of righteousness. It is a sign of God's spectacular grace that we are invited to think of ourselves as sheep and to think of God as our own shepherd.

But Jesus did not tell just one parable of lostness and the redeeming love of God. He proceeded to a second parable about a woman who had ten silver coins. Having lost one of them, she lit a lamp, swept the house, and sought diligently until she found it. Just as in the case of the lost sheep, Jesus began the parable by engaging the audience: Who among you wouldn't do exactly what this woman did as she sought the lost coin? If you lost something precious, wouldn't you seek after it? Once the woman found the coin, she called together her friends and neighbors and issued the same invitation as the shepherd of the previous parable: "Rejoice with me, for I have found the coin which I had lost!" Her joy far exceeded the sorrow she felt over losing the coin. What was precious before becomes even more precious now; the experience of losing it and finding it magnified its value to her. And, once again, the celebration is a picture of the "joy in the presence of the angels of God over one sinner who repents."

These two parables alone would have been an overwhelming rebuke to the Pharisees and scribes for grumbling about Jesus' proximity to tax collectors and sinners. The rebuke goes to the heart of the issue—the Pharisees and scribes really didn't care about lost people at all. They had no concern for bringing the lost sheep of Israel into the fold. They were adamantly determined to prove and protect their own righteousness by keeping their distance from sinners. As far as they were concerned, the lost could stay lost. They had convinced themselves that God was pleased with their self-righteousness. But according to Jesus they were tragically deluded.

And yet, Jesus wasn't finished. He'd defanged the critique of his earthly table fellowship with sinners and tax collectors, revealing himself to be a good shepherd who rejoices whenever one of his beloved sheep is found. And this effectively established a situation in which Jesus could deliver a third, much more powerful parable. It turns out that the parables of the lost sheep and the lost coin were ways of introducing the most powerful picture of all, the picture of a lost son.

We often refer to this passage as the "parable of the prodigal son." We must remember, however, that when we offer a name for a parable, we are also framing its interpretation. We must be careful that we name a parable in a way that is faithful to the entirety of the passage. The first sentence of this passage should awaken us to the fact that this is not a parable about a lost son; it is a parable about two sons. Furthermore, the central character in the parable is neither of the sons, but rather the father. Helmut Thielicke, a twentieth-century German preacher, referred to this passage as the "parable of the waiting father."[1] Thielicke is certainly right in pointing to the father as the central character in the passage, not the sons. And yet, our tendency to refer to it as the "parable of the prodigal son" indicates how easily we see ourselves in this younger son who acted so maliciously against his father, only to be received back with love and forgiveness. So we put ourselves in the center of the story. But properly speaking, God is always at the center of the story of salvation, even as it is God who is always at the center of the story of creation, for it is God who is the beginning and the middle and the end.

The passage proceeds by telling us that the younger of the two sons confronted his father with the nearly unthinkable demand that he be advanced the share of property that would come to him by inheritance. The background of this may be a bit complicated, but the moral thrust of the passage is abundantly clear. This son was effectively saying to his father that he wished he were dead. At the very least, the son was saying to his father that he was as good as dead to him, that he no longer wanted to be known as the man's son, that he wanted to stand on his own two feet with an inheritance that was not yet his by right, and that he intended to sever his relationship with the father in a way that was irreversible.

Theology professor and author Kenneth Bailey said that there is Talmudic evidence that a Jewish father could distribute property to his sons as an inheritance before death.[2] Nevertheless, the father was understood to have the right to live off of the proceeds of the estate until his death. The idea of receiving an inheritance in advance would probably have been familiar to those who heard Jesus tell the parable. But the audacity of the son absconding with the inheritance would have been beyond their imagination. In the case of the younger son, he committed a double treason—demanding the inheritance and then destroying the wealth. Both would have been seen as acts of hatred toward the father.

In any event, the father did divide the property between his two sons, with the older son receiving a significantly larger share of the inheritance than the younger. The younger son waited only a few days before gathering all he had, taking a journey into a far country, and there squandering his inheritance in what is described as "loose living." This narrative moves quite quickly, and Jesus did not offer any extraneous details. Although the older son later accused his brother of certain sinful acts, there is no statement at this point in the parable concerning specific behavior of the younger son. We just know that in short order he had destroyed the inheritance he had demanded from his father. It is a picture of utter recklessness, fecklessness, disrespect, treason, and criminal irresponsibility.

The entire logic of Israel was, in accordance with the law of God, to remain set apart from other nations. Therefore, a son of Israel moving to a foreign land represented not only treason against his family, but treason against the nation and against God himself, who had made a covenant with Israel. To add insult to injury, a severe famine came to the nation the son had taken refuge in, and now he was in danger of starving to death. Suddenly he found himself in a situation in which he was an alien without citizenship, without funds, and without hope. In desperation he hired himself out to one of the citizens of that pagan country, who sent him into his field to feed swine. The picture of utter degradation and violation of the law was now complete. There was almost nothing Jesus could add to this young man's crime and its consequences. Once a treasured son living safely in his father's house, his treasonous rebellion resulted in his living fatherless, homeless, nationless, and feeding swine. He eventually became so hungry that he was envious of the swine for the pods they were given to eat.

We know already that this is a picture of salvation. We knew that salvation was at stake with the lost lamb and with the lost coin, and now we see salvation at stake in the infinitely worse situation of a lost son. But the son was a conscious human being, with whom we can identify. When the lamb wandered off, it was merely doing what sheep do; the coin had no consciousness of its own lostness. The remarkable turn in this third parable is that the boy came to understand his treason. He came to terms with his own sin.

The Scripture elsewhere explains this as the convicting power of the Holy Spirit. Jesus described the conviction that came into the young man's heart as coming "to his senses." He came to a true knowledge of himself and of his condition. He saw himself for the traitor he was, and he understood his hopeless and helpless condition. Furthermore, he thought back to his father's house, envious now of his father's hired men who had "more than enough bread," even as he was dying of hunger in a foreign land. It occurred to him that he should return to his father, not to claim an identity as son, but merely to be hired on as a servant. He understood that being the hired servant of his father would be immeasurably greater than starving among swine.

The young man planned a speech for his father in which he would confess his sin and offer his solution: "Father, I have sinned against heaven, and in your sight. I am no longer worthy to be called your son; make me as one of your hired men." But Jesus said that when the son arose and returned to his father, the father saw him, felt compassion, ran and embraced him, and kissed him. (Note that the father's love is described as compassion, even as it was compassion that Jesus said was the motivating love of the Samaritan in another parable.)

Much has been made of the fact that the father ran to meet his son. Generally speaking, the person of a lower social status would run to meet a person of higher rank or position. In this case it was the son hesitantly returning home who was greeted by the father enthusiastically running to greet him. What a marvelous picture of the extravagant love of this father, pointing to the infinitely extravagant love of our heavenly Father toward us sinners.

The son made his confession, but he was interrupted before he could propose that his father take him on as a hired man. That confession was necessary. "Father, I have sinned against heaven and in your sight; I am no longer worthy to be called your son." Such confession is the fruit of repentance. The Holy Spirit works within the sinner's heart to bring about repentance, and that repentance brings the confession of sin, which is an essential part of our experience of salvation and the continuation of the Christian life. As the apostle John wrote, "If we confess our sins, he is faithful and just to forgive us our sins and to cleanse us from all unrighteousness" (1 John 1:9).

After his son's confession, the father showed his authority when he told his servants to bring the symbols of sonship—"the best robe and put it on him, and put a ring on his hand and sandals on his feet; and bring the fattened calf, kill it, and let us eat and celebrate." The father immediately established that he was receiving his son back *as his son*. It is the father who determines the status of those who are his sons. It is the father who has the authority to bestow the robe and the ring and the shoes. It is the father who holds the exclusive right to determine who will live in his household and be known as his own.

The gospel of Christ, depicted so memorably in this parable, reveals the magnificent and unexpected truth that we sinners (who deserve nothing but God's wrath) are received by him in Christ as sons, and with Christ we are made joint heirs by adoption (Rom. 8:17). This parable is not just about this lost son, but about every lost sinner who repents, confesses sin, and turns to the Father through Christ and his absolute grace.

The father's invitation for his friends to celebrate follows the example of the shepherd who had found his lamb and the woman who had found her coin, but there is far more at stake here. The father called for celebration because his son "was dead and has come to life again; he was lost and has been found." The joy of the shepherd and the joy of the woman are vastly eclipsed by the joy of this father. His son was not merely lost; he was effectively dead—but now he was alive. This is the experience of every sinner who comes to salvation in Christ. We were lost and now we are found, we were dead and now we are alive.

These three parables describe lostness, foundness, and rejoicing. The pattern is so clear that we know the father is going to call for rejoicing because he has received back his son. Those who love the father will love the son, and those who love the father will join him in rejoicing. And the cause of this rejoicing is greater than any other imaginable. A son who was dead is now alive. As Luke tells us, "They began to celebrate." At this point we have absolute parallels between these three parables of lostness that end in rejoicing. Those who had gathered near Jesus because of their own sense of lostness must have been hanging on every word. When Jesus told this third parable, we can just wonder how many of the tax collectors and sinners who had come near him heard the gospel and understood that Jesus was inviting them to come home. But we can also imagine the Pharisees and scribes who were already grumbling about Jesus realizing that they now had a great deal more about which to grumble. Through these parables, Jesus had told them that those who refuse to rejoice when that which was lost has been found are not friends of God at all. Their grumbling was a sign that they were themselves outside of the kingdom. To be in the kingdom, as in heaven, was to respond with rejoicing when sinners repent.

But of course, the third parable did not end at this point. In a stunning turn of events, Jesus shifted the narrative to the older son who was working in the field. As the older son came near to the house, he heard the unmistakable noise of celebration, music, and dancing. Rather than go to his father to find the cause of the celebration and join it, he instead called one of the servants and demanded an explanation. The servant responded, "Your brother has come, and your father has killed the fattened calf because he has received him back safe and sound." In response to this amazing news, the older son became angry and refused to go in.

The older brother's refusal to join in the celebration, similar to the Pharisees and scribes refusing to celebrate when sinners came near to Jesus in order to hear the good news of the gospel, is a picture of the ultimate and self-righteous delusion. The older son thought that he was bringing honor to the father by working in the field, but the condition of his heart indicated that he had no real intent to honor his father. His refusal to join in celebration over his brother's return became the unmistakable sign that he never really loved his father at all.

The parable of the prodigal son is not about one but two lost sons. The Pharisees and scribes would have been sufficiently incensed by the parable of one lost son who has been found and received back home, but this parable is clearly about the universality of human sin. The elder son was just as lost as the younger son, though he believed himself to deserve a place in the father's home. His refusal to celebrate indicates that in his heart he was as distant from the father as the younger son was in the lowest point of his rebellion.

The father went out to the older son, much as he had gone out to the younger son. We're told that the father entreated the son to join the celebration, but the son would have none of it. Instead, the son rebuked his own father, insisting that it was he who had served the father, never disobeyed his command, and yet was never even given a goat so that he might celebrate with his friends. "But when this son of yours came, who has devoured your wealth with prostitutes, you killed the fattened calf for him!" The youngest son committed treason by treating the father as if he were dead, taking his inheritance, and then squandering it in a foreign country. The older son showed an even more treacherous treason by continuing to live in the father's house while despising the father's heart. He assigned the basest of motives to the younger brother and insulted the father with his own argument of self-righteousness.

The final words belong to the father: "Son, you have always been with me, and all that is mine is yours. But we had to celebrate and rejoice, for this brother of yours was dead and has begun to live, and was lost and has been found."

If we hate the Father, we will always hate those who belong to the Father. If we love the Father, we will celebrate as the Father celebrates. If we truly love the Father, we will see all of those who belong to the Father as precious and welcome them when they come to the Father through faith and repentance. Our refusal to celebrate indicates a refusal to repent of sin and accept that very grace. The entreating words of the Father remain an invitation to the elder son to repent, to come and join the celebration and to be glad.

It is fitting that the Father in his sovereignty has the last word. Jesus was on his way to the cross, to die as a substitute and pay the penalty for our sin. Having just shared this parable with the grumbling scribes and Pharisees, it is as if Jesus was saying to them that there was still time to join the celebration as part of the kingdom of heaven. However, the unfolding Gospel of Luke after this parable tells us that the Pharisees and the scribes became even more hardened in their hearts. The self-righteousness displayed by the elder brother in this parable, and by the scribes and Pharisees, is hardly limited to them.

One of the marks of our own age is the eclipse of the sense of lostness. In modern times, efforts have been made to redefine the human problem as anything but being lost in rebellion against the one true God. Most people living in our secular society know they are lost in some sense, but they deny the truth that they are rebels against God himself.

The modern age has brought all kinds of alternative diagnoses. Karl Marx said that the problem of modern humanity is that we are alienated from our labor by the rise of the Industrial Revolution and the wage system. His answer was revolution. Sigmund Freud said that we are the victims of our own subconscious, and that salvation can come only by psychotherapy. The existentialist philosophers said that human beings face a crisis of authenticity, alienated from our true selves. Their argument was that relief can come only by actualizing the self as our own creation. All of these are efforts to avoid the truth about us, which is that we are rebels against God who like the younger son in this third parable have committed nothing less than treason. It is not that we are alienated from ourselves or alienated from our labor or alienated from our authenticity—it is that we are alienated from

God. The invitation remains for the sinner to come home, and it is an invitation addressed in this parable to both the older and the younger lost sons.

The precious promise of the gospel is this: "But now in Christ Jesus you who once were far off have been brought near by the blood of Christ" (Eph. 2:13).

# 7

# What Will He Do to Those Tenants?

## THE PARABLE OF THE TWO SONS AND THE PARABLE OF THE WICKED TENANTS

"What do you think? A man had two sons. And he went to the first and said, 'Son, go and work in the vineyard today.' And he answered, 'I will not,' but afterward he changed his mind and went. And he went to the other son and said the same. And he answered, 'I go, sir,' but did not go. Which of the two did the will of his father?" They said, "The first." Jesus said to them, "Truly, I say to you, the tax collectors and the prostitutes go into the kingdom of God before you. For John came to you in the way of righteousness, and you did not believe him, but the tax collectors and the prostitutes believed him. And even when you saw it, you did not afterward change your minds and believe him."

"Hear another parable. There was a master of a house who planted a vineyard and put a fence around it and dug a winepress in it and built a tower and leased it to tenants, and went into another country. When the season for fruit drew near, he sent his servants to the tenants to get his fruit. And the tenants took his servants and beat one, killed another, and stoned another. Again he sent other servants, more than the first. And they did the same to them. Finally he sent his son to them, saying, 'They will respect my son.' But when the tenants saw the son, they said to themselves, 'This is the heir. Come, let us kill him and have his inheritance.' And they took him and threw him out of the vineyard and killed him. When therefore the owner of the vineyard comes, what will he do to those tenants?" They said to him, "He will put those wretches to a miserable death and let out the vineyard to other tenants who will give him the fruits in their seasons."

Jesus said to them, "Have you never read in the Scriptures:

"'The stone that the builders rejected
has become the cornerstone;
this was the Lord's doing,
and it is marvelous in our eyes'?

"Therefore I tell you, the kingdom of God will be taken away from you and given to a people producing its fruits. And the one who falls on this stone will be broken to pieces; and when it falls on anyone, it will crush him." (Matt. 21:28–44)

As Jesus entered Jerusalem for the last time, he made his way to the temple. Those words alone are sufficient to indicate the heightened tension of the situation, even without our knowledge of the coming conflict. Jesus knew, as we now know, what lay ahead. He would be arrested, tried, tortured, crucified, and then on the third day he would rise from the dead. The tension in Matthew 21 was so high that it must have been nearly unbearable for those, including the disciples, who were with Jesus. The stage was set for the most dramatic and significant events in all of human history.

By the time we come to Matthew 21, Jesus had not only entered Jerusalem, but he had entered the temple. As he was teaching in the temple, the chief priests and the elders of the people came up to challenge him. Specifically, they challenged his authority to teach: "By what authority are you doing these things, and who gave you this authority?" (v. 23). Before looking at how Jesus responded to this insolent question, let's understand what was really happening here. The Son of God incarnate, the Divine Logos through whom the world was made, the Messiah who would sit forever on David's throne, the Son of Man sent for the salvation of his people, God in human flesh, was being accosted by those who believed themselves to be the true authorities in the temple.

It is far too easy to focus on the words of Jesus found in a text like this without giving adequate attention to the context. Understand exactly what is taking place in this passage: not merely a horrifying display of human arrogance, but an unforgivable act of treason that takes place in the precincts of the temple.

Jesus immediately subverted their authority by taking charge of the conversation. He refused to answer their question unless they would answer his own: "I also will ask you one question, and if you tell me the answer, then I will tell you by what authority I do these things," said Jesus (v. 24). The question Jesus asked will surprise us, as it undoubtedly surprised the chief priests and the elders. Jesus asked about the baptism of John, specifically, "From where did it come? From heaven or from man?" (v. 25).

Jesus was not asking a question of arcane theological interest. He was not asking a question that was calculated to test the theological acumen or biblical knowledge of the chief priests and the elders. He knew, and they knew, that he was asking them a question that would reveal the essence of their hearts and would also put them, standing before the people and the temple, in the position where they would have to acknowledge either that John the Baptist had been sent by God or that he was a false prophet.

We can imagine the anxiety among the elders and the chief priests as they discussed among themselves how they could possibly answer the question. They clearly understood their predicament. If they declared John the Baptist to be from God, then they would have to explain why they had refused his call to repentance. On the other hand, if they identified John the Baptist as a false prophet, they would place themselves against the people, who had the common biblical sense to understand that John was indeed a prophet sent from God. Jesus put them in this predicament in such a way that they experienced it not only privately, in conversation with Jesus, but publicly as they stood before the people in the temple.

The temple authorities discussed the question and understood their options clearly: "If we say, 'From heaven,' he will say to us, 'Why then did you not believe him?' But if we say, 'From man,' we are afraid of the crowd, for they all hold that John was a prophet" (vv. 25–26). They had correctly identified their two options and the consequences of answering either way. They spoke candidly of the fact that they were afraid of the crowd. But if they acknowledged that he'd been sent from heaven, that haunting question would hang over them. In truth, it hangs over them even today: "Why then did you not believe him?" (v. 25).

In an ultimate act of surrender combined with naked cowardice, the temple authorities simply answered Jesus, "We do not know." Jesus responded, "Neither will I tell you by what authority I do these things" (v. 27).

*We do not know.*

It is sobering to recognize that hell will be filled with people who said, "We do not know." But they will be in hell because they *did* know. This is exactly what the apostle Paul underlined in Romans 1 when he spoke of God's revelation of himself: "For what can be known about God is plain to them, because God has shown it to them. For his invisible attributes, namely, his eternal power and divine nature, had been clearly perceived, ever since the creation of the world, in the things that have been made. So they are without excuse" (vv. 19–20).

Paul made abundantly clear that there is no one who does not know enough about God to be held accountable. There is no one in hell who will be there who can truly use the excuse that he or she did not know. This feigned ignorance is itself a sign of spiritual rebellion. Paul made that clear when he followed his affirmation of God's universal revelation with this judgment: "For although they knew God, they did not honor him as God or give thanks to him, but they became futile in their thinking, and their foolish hearts were darkened. Claiming to be wise, they became fools, and exchanged the glory of the immortal God for images resembling mortal man and birds and animals and creeping things" (vv. 21–23).

Throughout biblical history, the statement "we do not know" is almost always false. It is especially false in the case of the temple authorities who could not answer Jesus' question. Perhaps it's better to say, they *would* not answer his question.

Jesus simply responded to their statement of ignorance by refusing to answer their question, and thus refusing their authority. He said to them, "Neither will I tell you by what authority I do these things" (Matt. 21:27).

This confrontation in the temple was a sign of things to come. The abdication of responsibility on the part of the chief priests and the elders was indicative of the kind of abdicated responsibility we will see in the Gospel of John when Pilate simply asked, "What is truth?" and then washed his hands of the matter (18:38). When people respond to the gospel of Jesus Christ with this kind of intellectual resignation, they send their souls to hell.

This passage's record of the encounter between the temple authorities and Jesus sets the stage for two parables that are direct rebukes of the Jewish establishment in Jerusalem. In the parable of the two sons and the parable of the wicked tenants, Jesus offered the most severe and unflinching indictment of Israel's refusal to acknowledge him as Lord, Messiah, and King.

It's a horrible thing to deny the ministry of John the Baptist. It's an infinitely more horrible thing to deny the authority and ministry of the Lord Jesus Christ. The fact it happened in the temple points to the almost unspeakable horror of the denial. And make no mistake, the temple authorities knew exactly what they were doing and they, representing the Jewish establishment, just became more obstinate in their defiance of Jesus. Remember, they would soon demand that he be crucified.

## The Parable of the Two Sons

When we think about Jesus telling a parable of two sons, our minds almost automatically go to what we commonly identify as the "parable of the prodigal son." As we have seen, it is a parable about two lost sons, with the elder brother in that parable representing the Jewish establishment and the pattern of their rejection of Jesus.

Matthew's parable is much shorter than the parable of the prodigal son, but it is spoken directly to the temple authorities and the chief priests so that there would be no mistaking whom Jesus was indicting here.

Jesus introduced his audience to a man who had two sons. We have seen previously that when Jesus began by speaking of "a certain rich man," he knew that his hearers would have a negative image. The opposite is true here, for to the Jewish ears of the time, the statement that a man had two sons would be heard as a reflection of God's blessing.

In Jesus' parable, this man went to the first son, who as the firstborn would be considered the heir of the father's estate and the chief instrument of the father's continuation through future generations, and said, "Go and work in the vineyard today." Astoundingly, the son answered, "I will not." At this point, those hearing the parable would understand the sinfulness of the disobedience represented in the son's refusal to obey the father. He sounded like a defiant toddler. But we're told, after having declared his disobedience, he changed his mind and went to work in the vineyard. Thus far, this seems to be little more than an awkward family moment, but as you might suspect, there is more to come.

Having heard his first son's disobedient response, the father went to his other son and also told him to go to the vineyard and work. The second son said, "I go, sir." That's certainly a good start. The younger son indicated obedience rather than disobedience—but Jesus shared that he "did not go."

Here we have two sons who seemed to represent a dysfunctional family. The son who verbally refused his father's instruction ended up obeying him after all, while the son who immediately and respectfully promised to obey failed to do so. Jesus then asked the question of those hearing the parable: "Which of the two did the will of his father?"

Now remember Jesus told this parable to the disciples but also to the chief priests and the elders of the people. Matthew made clear that the parable is a part of Jesus' response to the priests' and elders' arrogant challenge to his authority. But don't forget that there were people watching and listening to this confrontation. So when Jesus asked them the question, "Which of the two did the will of the father?" all the people heard the priests and elders answer correctly that the first son was the one who had ultimately obeyed.

Of course, they were right. Jesus revealed that it is not how one answers with words but how one answers with action that matters in the end. The truest picture of obedience would be to answer rightly and then act rightly as well. But Jesus has a subversive point to make here—subversive, that is, of the authority of the chief priests and the elders. After they answered the question, Jesus rebuked the chief priests and the elders of the temple yet again: "Truly, I say to you. The tax collectors and the prostitutes go into the kingdom of God before you. For John came to you in the way of righteousness, and you did not believe him, but tax collectors and the prostitutes believed him. And even when you saw it, you did not afterward change your minds and believe him."

This stinging rebuke from Jesus is a continuation of his rebuke to their question about his authority. There can be no question who had the authority in the temple this day, for it was Jesus who was judging the chief priests and the elders, not the other way around. Jesus would not be judged by them. They were in no position to judge Jesus. And Jesus lay on them the indictment that they had rejected God's messenger and refused to hear the truth or repent of their sin—a pattern that started long before Jesus' public ministry.

It is almost impossible for Christians today to understand the startling nature of the rebuke that Jesus offered to these temple authorities when he told them, "The tax collectors and the prostitutes go into the kingdom of God before you." This was beyond the theological imagination of the temple authorities, and that was the problem. Like the Pharisee in the parable of the Pharisee and the tax collector of Luke 18, they trusted in their own righteousness, believed their own propaganda, and had convinced themselves that they were theologically and spiritually superior and thus would be first in the kingdom. Now, Jesus told them that if they were ever to enter the kingdom at all, it would be behind the tax collectors and the prostitutes.

But before we leave this parable, we need to understand that Jesus was accusing the chief priests and the elders of being neither the first nor the second son in his short parable. Unlike the first son who stated disobedience and then obeyed, or the second son who stated obedience but then disobeyed, these Jewish leaders combined the worst components of both sons. As Jesus told them, they did not believe John, and the Jewish authorities did not "afterward change [their] minds and believe him." They stated their disobedience, and they obstinately remained in their disobedience. In effect, they showed themselves to be no sons of God at all.

## The Parable of the Wicked Tenants

The stage was now set for Jesus to follow the first parable with a second, which would bring even greater specificity and intensity to the conflict with the priests and elders. This is similar to the cycle of parables we find in Luke 15, the parables of lostness and foundness. In those stories, Luke revealed three parables to us, each with increasing intensity and significance. We move from a lost lamb to a lost coin to lost sons. In Matthew 21, the rising intensity takes us from two sons whose father owned a vineyard, to a much more explosive story of a vineyard that reveals the absolute rejection of the Son of God. Further, this parable revealed that the Jewish leaders' rejection would be met with the greatest display of the Father's affirmation of the Son and the most devastating judgment against those who refused to believe.

Jesus began his story with the master of the house who had planted a vineyard. He put a fence around it, dug a winepress in it, and even built a tower—clearly a man of significant wealth. His vineyard was a demonstration of his dominion. He not only planted the vineyard but he hedged it about with the fence. Digging a winepress meant that he could follow the grape all the way from the vine to its final product. In order to guard the vineyard from enemies, both animals and humans, he built a tower for observation. At this point, it is useful to look back to the Old Testament and recall that God referred to Israel as his beloved vineyard through the prophet Isaiah. Isaiah 5 speaks of God's tender nurturing love for his vineyard and expresses that love in extremely personal terms. And yet, the vineyard becomes the arena for a rebellion against the vineyard owner, and the vines yield only wild grapes:

> Let me sing for my beloved
>> my love song concerning his vineyard:
> My beloved had a vineyard
>> on a very fertile hill.
> He dug it and cleared it of stones,
>> and planted it with choice vines;
> he built a watchtower in the midst of it,
>> and hewed out a wine vat in it;
> and he looked for it to yield grapes,
>> but it yielded wild grapes.
> And now, O inhabitants of Jerusalem
>> and men of Judah,

judge between me and my vineyard.
What more was there to do for my vineyard,
    that I have not done in it?
When I looked for it to yield grapes,
    why did it yield wild grapes?
And now I will tell you
    what I will do to my vineyard.
I will remove its hedge,
    and it shall be devoured;
I will break down its wall,
    and it shall be trampled down.
I will make it a waste;
    it shall not be pruned or hoed,
    and briers and thorns shall grow up;
I will also command the clouds
    that they rain no rain upon it.
For the vineyard of the LORD of hosts
    is the house of Israel,
and the men of Judah
    are his pleasant planting;
and he looked for justice,
    but behold, bloodshed;
for righteousness,
    but behold, an outcry!

(VV. 1-7)

The language used here is among the sweetest poetry in the Old Testament. The Lord spoke of his vineyard with a love song. As in Jesus' parable, the vineyard is described as having been carefully planted and lovingly tended. And as also in the parable, Isaiah wrote of a watchtower that was built in the midst of this vineyard and of the wine vat that was built in expectation of the vineyard's harvest.

Poignantly, God asked, "What more was there to do for my vineyard, that I have not done it? When I looked for it to yield grapes, why did it yield wild grapes?"

Israel understood the divine judgment that was delivered in those questions. What more could God have done for Israel? Isaiah 5 is clearly in the background of Jesus' parable in Matthew 21. But in the case of Jesus' parable, the sin is not so much wild grapes as it is outright rebellion on the part of the people who claimed to be the great stewards of Israel's temple.

This indictment became clear when Jesus explained that when the time of harvest approached, the master of the house sent his servants to the tenants in order to get his fruit from the harvest. Shockingly, we learn that the tenants abused his servants terribly: "They beat one, killed another, and stoned another." Jesus added, "Again he sent other servants, more than the first. And they did the same to them." This pattern of beating and killing and stoning is a graphic but true description of the way Israel responded to so many of the prophets of God.

Just think about Stephen's declaration during his trial by some of the same authorities: "You stiff-necked people, uncircumcised in heart and ears, you always resist the Holy Spirit. As your fathers did, so do you. Which of the prophets did your fathers not persecute? And they killed those who announced beforehand the coming of the Righteous One, whom you have now betrayed and murdered, you who received the law as delivered by angels and did not keep it" (Acts 7:51–53). Stephen's indictment came with such a sting, but it comes on the other side of the death, burial, and resurrection of the Lord Jesus Christ. By then, those who accused Jesus in the temple had accomplished their plot to kill him.

At this point in the parable, the vineyard owner had sent numerous servants into the vineyard in order to claim his rightful harvest. Those he sent had been beaten, stoned, and killed. So the lord of the vineyard came to the conclusion that he would send his son to the wicked tenants, since his son would represent his own authority. The logic of the lord of the vineyard was clear: "They will respect my son." This would be the vineyard owner's rightful expectation. To mistreat the son of the vineyard owner would be a far more extreme act of rebellion and treason than mistreating his servants.

Nevertheless, we know that the wicked tenants treated the son with an even deeper hatred than the servants they had beaten, stoned, and killed. They saw their opportunity to take possession of the vineyard and commit grand larceny. "This is the heir. Come, let us kill him and have his inheritance," they said. Fulfilling their plot, the wicked tenants took the son, threw him out of the vineyard, and killed him.

This is exactly what the Jewish authorities would eventually do to Jesus.

Remember that Jesus was telling this parable to those who had questioned his authority. He had already indicted them with the question they could not answer. He followed that with the denunciation of the fact that they had rebelled against God by rejecting the message of John the Baptist. Then he amplified his indictment with the parable of the two sons, showing the double nature of Israel's disobedience. Now he accused the Jewish authorities, the chief priests and the leaders of the temple, of plotting his own murder.

Next, Jesus put the ultimate question to the Jewish authorities listening to his parable: "When therefore the owner of the vineyard comes, what will he do to those tenants?" This was an unavoidable question. The Jewish authorities quickly said to him, "He will put those wretches to a miserable death and let out the vineyard to other tenants who will give him the fruits in their seasons."

The chief priests and the elders of the people had answered correctly. They had no choice but to offer the right answer. The situation Jesus described was so extreme that the ultimate punishment and vengeance was the only right response and proper recourse of the vineyard owner. The tenants were murderers who must pay the price for their murder. They were traitors who must pay the price for their treason.

At this point, Jesus responded to them once again with the Scriptures. "Have you never read in the Scriptures," Jesus asked, "'The stone that the builders rejected has become the cornerstone; this was the Lord's doing and it is marvelous in our eyes'?" Jesus was quoting from Psalm 118:22–23. He was describing himself as the cornerstone that the builders had rejected. Those who considered themselves the builders and the rightful authorities in the temple were being told that the very stone they had rejected had become the cornerstone. Clearly, Jesus was reaching back to the Psalms in order to announce that he was himself that rejected stone. This is indeed God's doing and it is indeed marvelous in the eyes of all who love God.

This revelation of Jesus Christ as the cornerstone becomes an important theme in the entire New Testament. Paul, writing to the Ephesians, would describe the church as "the household of God, built on the foundation of the apostles and prophets, Christ Jesus himself being the cornerstone, in whom the whole structure, being joined together, grows into a holy temple in the Lord. In him you are also being built together into a dwelling place for God by the Spirit" (Eph. 2:19–22). Paul was describing the church as built upon Christ as the chief cornerstone that holds the entire structure together and is, as the people of God, "a holy temple in the Lord."

In the Old Testament, the prophet Isaiah had declared that God had laid in Zion a foundation stone, "a precious cornerstone" (Isa. 28:16), and the apostle Peter, building on Isaiah's texts, declared that this chief cornerstone is none other than Jesus Christ. Putting together the reference to Christ as cornerstone in Isaiah and in the Psalms, Peter declared that Christ as the cornerstone of the church is precious, but the cornerstone is also "a stone of stumbling and a rock of offense" (1 Peter 2:8).

This takes us back to the parable where Jesus declared to the temple authorities and the chief priests that the kingdom of God will be taken away from them "and given to a people producing its fruits." But now, Jesus pressed the case further: "And the one who falls on this stone will be broken to pieces; and when it falls on anyone, it will crush him." Daniel had warned of the days in which the God of Israel would break the disobedient into pieces. In Daniel 2:44–45, Daniel wrote, "And in the days of those kings the God of heaven will set up a kingdom that shall never be destroyed, nor shall the kingdom be left to another people. It shall break in pieces all these kingdoms and bring them to an end, and it shall stand forever, just as you saw that a stone was cut from a mountain by no human hand, and that it broke in pieces the iron, the bronze, the clay, the silver, and the gold. A great God has made known to the king what shall be after this."

Jesus presented himself clearly as the fulfillment of these Old Testament prophecies and promises. But these Old Testament passages come as both promise to the faithful and as eternal judgment to the unfaithful. Jesus came in order to save, but he would also crush to pieces those who oppose him.

This reminds us of what is at stake in the gospel of Jesus Christ. It is not just the promise of salvation, though that is the great message that makes the gospel such good news. It is also a word of warning to those who reject Christ. One of the most consistent themes of the parables is that those who reject Jesus will face a judgment that will lead to weeping and gnashing of teeth. In Matthew 21 Jesus told the chief priests and the elders of the people with unmistakable clarity that the cornerstone would fall on them and that they would be utterly crushed.

And yet, the chief priests and the elders of the people were so hard-hearted and obstinate that they did not receive the message. Matthew tells us, "When the chief priests and the Pharisees heard his parables, they perceived that he was speaking about them. And although they were seeking to arrest him, they feared the crowds, because they held him to be a prophet" (21:45–46). This is an absolutely pathetic observation. The chief priests and the Pharisees heard the parables, but they would not *hear* them even as Jesus had just laid them low with a message of destruction and an eternal verdict. Even though Jesus had been as clear as possible in his parable and in his direct words of judgment, they still refused to see the obvious.

These two parables come in the course of the Gospel of Matthew revealing the fulfillment of the Scripture in the rejection of the Messiah. These two parables bring words of almost unspeakable judgment against Israel. Make no mistake: Jesus Christ, the chief cornerstone, will save all who turn to him, but those who refuse will be broken to pieces and crushed. As Jesus was headed to the cross in order to save sinners, he made abundantly clear just what was at stake.

# 8

## Unworthy Guests

### THE PARABLE OF THE WEDDING FEAST

Let us rejoice and exult and give him the glory, for the marriage of the Lamb has come, and his Bride has made herself ready.

—REVELATION 19:7

The Spirit and the Bride say, "Come." And let the one who hears say, "Come." And let the one who is thirsty come; let the one who desires take the water of life without price.

—REVELATION 22:17

"Come, everyone who thirsts, come to the waters; and he who has no money, come, buy and eat!"

—ISAIAH 55:1

Jesus spoke to them again in parables, saying, "The kingdom of heaven may be compared to a king who gave a wedding feast for his son. And he sent out his slaves to call those who had been invited to the wedding feast, and they were unwilling to come. Again he sent out other slaves saying, 'Tell those who have been invited, "Behold, I have prepared my dinner; my oxen and my fattened livestock are all butchered and everything is ready; come to the wedding feast."' But they paid no attention and went their way, one to his own farm, another to his business, and the rest seized his slaves and mistreated them and killed them. But the king was enraged, and he sent his armies and destroyed those murderers and set their city on fire. Then he said to his slaves, 'The wedding is ready, but those who were invited were not worthy. Go therefore to the main highways, and as many as you find there, invite to the wedding feast.' Those slaves went out into the streets and gathered together all they found, both evil and good; and the wedding hall was filled with dinner guests.

"But when the king came in to look over the dinner guests, he saw a man there who was not dressed in wedding clothes, and he said to him, 'Friend, how did you come in here without wedding clothes?' And the man was speechless. Then the king said to the servants, 'Bind him hand and foot, and throw him into the outer darkness; in that place there will be weeping and gnashing of teeth.' For many are called, but few are chosen." (Matt. 22:1–14 NASB95)

There is nothing quite like a royal wedding. With the advent of television, royal weddings now draw many millions of viewers worldwide. There are multiple causes for this fascination, but it boils down to the fact that a royal wedding brings together the joy of a wedding celebration with the fascination we have with power and pageantry. This is exactly what we confront in Jesus' parable of the wedding feast. According to Matthew, as Jesus was speaking many things in parables, he compared the kingdom of God to a king who gave a wedding feast for his son. The slaves were sent to call those who were on the official wedding list, but they would not come. This sets up a most unexpected and illuminating picture of the reality of human sin and the magnificence of the grace of God. It also points to something that becomes a central motif of Scripture and the Christian life. The kingdom of God is a kingdom of joy. The kingdom of heaven is marked by absolute peace—not merely the peace that means the cessation of active hostility, but the peace that means the establishment of the benevolent rule of God. The kingdom of heaven means the perfection of life under the absolute rule of the perfect God—Father, Son, and Holy Spirit. To be a part of this kingdom is the greatest joy a human being can ever know, and the refusal to enter God's kingdom by invitation and to experience the joy of the king is inexcusable treason.

The host was not just any father, nor the groom just any son. This was a royal event, an invitation that simply could not be rejected. Anyone listening to this parable would immediately understand the basic irrationality, unspeakable rudeness, and unthinkable stupidity of turning down this royal invitation. Yet, when the servants were sent out to deliver invitations to the wedding feast, those who were on the official list simply would not come.

Jesus would surely have had the attention of his entire audience at this point. Who among them would ever expect to be invited to such an occasion—and who could imagine turning down such an opportunity?

The king sent another group of slaves, telling them to make clear the extent of the celebration, the magnificence of the affair, and the fact that each guest was personally invited to the wedding feast. But, once again those who received invitations paid no attention and went off to attend to other concerns—very pedestrian concerns. One went to his farm. Another went to his business. These were the priorities that took precedence over a magnificent wedding feast for which oxen and fat calves had already been slaughtered. Everything was ready, but those who were on the invitation list had better things to do. Worse yet, some of those invited seized the slaves who had brought the invitations, treated them shamefully, and even killed them.

This is a pattern of behavior we have seen elsewhere in Scripture. This is exactly the kind of language used to describe the treatment of the prophets of God in the Old Testament. They were often treated shamefully. And Jesus himself, the Son of God, would soon be treated shamefully and killed. This response is beyond all reason. It's unthinkably rude to reject the royal invitation. But to treat the king's slaves shamefully, much less to kill them, represents an act of calculated violence against the crown. Whether in the first century or in our own times, this response is almost beyond our imagination. How *could* anyone act so shamefully? Why *would* anyone refuse such an invitation, much less murder those who announced it?

It would soon become clear that Jesus was getting our attention in order to tell us that this is exactly how he himself was being treated. The Gospel of John tells us that Jesus came to his own and his own received him not. We also know that Jesus was treated exactly like the slaves of the king described in this parable. When Jesus spoke these words, the attention of those who heard him would have been rapt and urgent.

The king's response in anger is fully understandable, as he sent his troops in order to establish order. He demonstrated his wrath by destroying those who had murdered his slaves and brought judgment upon the entire city by burning it. This picture of divine judgment is, once again, similar to what we see in the Old Testament, beginning with cities such as Sodom and Gomorrah. It is a picture of God's judgment poured out upon those who have, in every way imaginable, rejected his lordship and refused his kingdom.

But the parable was not over. In the remarkable words of verse 8, the king declared that "those who were invited were not worthy." He then told the servants to go out into the highways and invite anyone who passed by to the wedding feast, "as many as you find there." So the servants went out into the roads "and gathered together all they found, both evil and good," until the wedding hall was filled with guests.

We must be careful not to take every detail of this parable as having allegorical significance. We already know this is not the right way to read a parable. Rather, we are to understand the story told by Jesus in terms of its context and overall thrust. The context here is that Jesus was headed for the cross and there was rising treason against him. The scribes and the Pharisees, along with the chief priests and the temple authorities, were conspiring to kill him. Jesus had just told the parable of the wicked tenants, and the parable of the wedding feast followed immediately. Jesus had just warned those who were plotting his destruction that he was the cornerstone. He warned that "the one who falls on this stone will be broken to pieces; and when it falls on anyone, it will crush him" (Matt. 21:44). Jesus was pressing the point with this parable of the wedding feast, but he also made clear that there would be those who would hear the word of the gospel, believe that word, repent of their sins, and come into the great feast of God.

The point, then, is that it is the unlikely and unpredicted who will enter the kingdom, not those who believe themselves to be the earthly representatives of it. The chief priests and the Pharisees were plotting

Jesus' destruction, but there were yet those who would believe, repent of their sins, and enter into salvation.

There could be no doubt that Jesus was instructing the church to cast a wide net, inviting all persons to come to Christ for salvation. The wedding feast of the parable points ahead to the Great Feast, the joyful fulfillment and celebration of his kingdom. But this story should make us uncomfortable and even horrified at the brutality and evil of those who rejected the king's invitation. We should be humbled by the destruction that was visited upon them.

Consider also how the parable proceeds after the wedding hall was filled with guests. Jesus changed the trajectory of the parable to tell us that when the king came in to see his guests, he saw a man who was improperly dressed, wearing no wedding garment. There is more here than a cursory reading might suggest. It is not that this man had failed to wear some specific article of clothing appropriate for a wedding. Instead, he had clearly come to the party without intending to honor the king. He wanted the benefits of the feast without any acknowledgment of the king's sovereignty and graciousness. In this case the refusal to wear the garment represented an intentional effort to insult the king and to join the party under false pretenses. The king addressed the man, "Friend, how did you come in here without wedding clothes?" The man had no answer, so the king told his attendants to bind the man and cast him into "the outer darkness; in that place there will be weeping and gnashing of teeth." Jesus then concluded, "For many are called, but few are chosen."

We have to unpack this with care, lest we misconstrue the meaning of this parable. This is not a rebuke of someone who showed up merely with inadequate dress. This is someone who showed up as a direct affront to the king. This was not someone who responded graciously to the invitation given. This was someone who had come to insult the king while joining in the wedding feast. Don't miss that Jesus shared this parable immediately after sharing the parable of the wicked tenants. This is a continuation of the same point, with a different emphasis. Just as the wicked tenants killed the son in the prior parable, in this passage we see the king and the kingdom insulted by a man who came in without washing himself and getting himself ready for such a royal occasion. The words of judgment uttered here by the king are precisely the words of divine judgment that Jesus has used repeatedly to warn sinners: when the king sentences this man to be cast into the place where "there will be weeping and gnashing of teeth," we are looking at the same eternal, conscious punishment by the final decree of God that we see described and confirmed elsewhere in Scripture.

What are we to do with this parable? We need to understand how Jesus was blending together biblical theology and gospel invitation, a warning about the judgment that is to come and an invitation to sinners to join the feast of God. This is a parable that grabs our attention and will not let us go as it tells us of those who shamefully rejected the king's invitation to his son's wedding.

Reaching back into multiple themes from the Old Testament, Jesus' use of the image of a wedding feast is extraordinarily rich. The opening chapters of the book of Genesis reveal that marriage was one of the great climactic moments of creation. On the sixth day, God created human beings in his image. He created the woman out of man, the one for the other, making human beings in his image as male and female. The man and the woman in the garden were brought together in the institution of marriage, even as they were given the command to be fruitful and multiply and fill the earth.

The glory of God was especially revealed in the coming together of the man and the woman. Weddings are one of the two nearly universal human commemorations. In almost every society throughout history, there have been the commemorations of funerals and weddings. The first is the occasion for grief; the second is the occasion for unmitigated joy. There's something inherently right about a man and a woman coming together in marriage, making it an occasion for the entire community to celebrate. In the case of a royal wedding, the ceremony and the feast are an occasion for the entire nation to celebrate. As the king rejoices, the kingdom rejoices.

It is not insignificant that Jesus performed his first miracle at a wedding. To be invited to a wedding is to be invited to a festival celebration. To be invited to the wedding feast is an honor even beyond that of attending the ceremony itself.

God is hosting the great wedding of the Son and his bride, the church. It's not just biblical theology from the Old Testament that informs our understanding of this passage, but the comprehensive picture in the New Testament of the church as Christ's bride, adorned for the wedding with holiness. The eschatological vision of Scripture points to the marriage supper of the Lamb in Revelation 19. In that passage, we see the marriage supper of the Lamb announced with these words: "'Hallelujah! For the Lord our God the Almighty reigns. Let us rejoice and exult and give him the glory, for the marriage of the Lamb has come, and his Bride has made herself ready; it was granted her to clothe herself with fine linen bright and pure'—for the fine linen is the righteous deeds of the saints."

Furthermore, the angel said to John, "'Write this: Blessed are those who are invited to the marriage supper of the Lamb.' And he said to me, 'These are the true words of God'" (vv. 6–9).

The marriage supper of the Lamb thus becomes the great festival celebration of the fullness of the kingdom of God. The Lamb is worthy of worship, and his bride, the blood-bought church of the Lord Jesus Christ, is adorned with the righteous deeds of the saints, made holy in Christ. The great consummation of the kingdom is pictured as the consummation of the wedding between Christ and the church; and the great event, as in this parable, is the feast, the marriage supper.

As the angel said to John, "Blessed are those who are invited to the marriage supper of the Lamb." Who *could* refuse this invitation? Who *would* refuse this invitation? The sad reality is that there are many who refuse this invitation. This is why Jesus said at the end of the parable in Matthew 22, "For many are called, but few are chosen." That certainly points to the sovereignty of God in salvation, and it also points to the fact that those who respond are indeed those who are chosen. Those who come to Christ by faith are the ones whose hearts have been open to the gospel, who have been brought to conviction of sin, who know their need in Christ and have believed in him and repented of their sins.

There is grace in this parable. It reveals the power of the gospel. There are *none* worthy of salvation, and yet God will make certain that the wedding hall of the kingdom will be filled with guests. Grace is abundantly evident in this parable in the fact that the king issued his invitation and made everything ready for his guests. God has in Christ accomplished everything necessary for our salvation.

But there's also judgment in this parable. It points to the hard-heartedness of humanity and the refusal to accept God's invitation. That act of refusal, far beyond run-of-the-mill rudeness, comes with eternal consequences. God's judgment is just. Many who refuse to come are on the "A list" of invitees. Many who will celebrate at the marriage supper of the Lamb will be those whom no human authority would have invited but have nonetheless been brought near to God through Christ. They heard the invitation and came.

Finally, this parable also points to the exclusivity of the gospel. Those who attend the great wedding feasts of the kingdom will be those who heard the gospel of Jesus Christ and believed in him by faith. Salvation comes only by God's grace *alone* through faith in Christ *alone*. This same gospel is the very gospel that we are assigned to preach to all the nations, indeed on the highways and in the hedges. The church's commission is twofold: to announce this invitation to the ends of the earth, and to join in the celebration of the king's love and grace. This is our charge until that day when we are welcomed to the marriage supper of the Lamb.

Until then, we have much work to do—and much joy to share!

# 9

# When the Son of Man Comes, Will He Find Faith on Earth?

## THE PARABLE OF THE PERSISTENT WIDOW

> Now faith is the assurance of things hoped for, the conviction of things not seen. For by it the people of old received their commendation. By faith we understand that the universe was created by the word of God, so that what is seen was not made of the things that are visible.
>
> —HEBREWS 11:1–3

> For by grace you have been saved through faith. And this is not your own doing; it is the gift of God, not as a result of works, so that no one may boast.
>
> —EPHESIANS 2:8–9

And he told them a parable to the effect that they ought always to pray and not lose heart. He said, "In a certain city there was a judge who neither feared God nor respected man. And there was a widow in that city who kept coming to him and saying, 'Give me justice against my adversary.' For a while he refused, but afterward he said to himself, 'Though I neither fear God nor respect man, yet because this widow keeps bothering me, I will give her justice, so that she will not beat me down by her continual coming.'" And the Lord said, "Hear what the unrighteous judge says. And will not God give justice to his elect, who cry to him day and night? Will he delay long over them? I tell you, he will give justice to them speedily. Nevertheless, when the Son of Man comes, will he find faith on earth?" (Luke 18:1–8)

In the first verses of Luke 18 we encounter one of the most interesting characters found anywhere in Scripture. She is simply described as a persistent widow. But, make no mistake, her persistence is extraordinary, and Christ presents her as a model of Christian faithfulness. It turns out that the persistent widow is one of the most steadfast characters in all of Scripture. But she earned that reputation by driving a wicked judge nearly insane.

We've seen how often Jesus' parables have the power to catch us by surprise. The woman described in this parable is not the predictable sort of heroine we're used to encountering in stories: She was a nameless widow, counted among the most powerless in society. She was not rewarded for doing anything great in and of itself, but merely for her persistence in demanding justice from an unfaithful judge.

Luke began this parable with the statement: "And he told them a parable to the effect that they ought always to pray and not lose heart." We do not have that kind of introductory statement for every parable, but in this case Luke wanted us to know that the point Jesus was making was that Christians are to be persistent in prayer and not lose heart. We're to trust God, turning to him in the knowledge that he will respond in a way that is consistent with his loving character and sovereign power. But, he will answer our prayers on his own timetable and in a way that brings him greatest glory.

Jesus did not begin the parable by introducing the widow, but by introducing the judge who "neither feared God nor respected man." This is about as severe an indictment of judicial malfeasance as we can imagine. This was a judge who wasn't about justice at all. He didn't fear God. He did not recognize his own judicial responsibilities as an extension of God's justice and mercy. Nor did he follow or respect even human understandings of justice and the judiciary. To the contrary, he feared no one and respected no one, which is a recipe for disaster.

Nevertheless, Jesus quickly introduced the fact that there was a widow in the same city who kept coming to this judge demanding justice. "Give me justice against my adversary," she demanded. We're told that for a while the judge refused but eventually he was worn down by the widow's persistence. In an amazing statement of self-knowledge he said, "Though I neither fear God nor respect man, yet because this widow keeps bothering me, I will give her justice, so that she will not beat me down by her continual coming."

It's easy to see how the woman became identified as the "persistent widow." She simply would not give up. Her only human rescue could come by means of this judge, who bore the responsibility to execute judgment. She had a righteous cause and she knew it, and she pressed it against this judge who, fearing and respecting neither God nor man, was unmoved by the merits of her claim and the justness of her cause.

Instead, he was worn down by her persistence. He referred to how she had beaten him down "by her continual coming." And make no mistake, this widow would have come again and again and again until she had obtained justice.

Jesus brought the short parable to a tidy conclusion with the words, "Hear what the unrighteous judge says. And will not God give justice to his elect, who cry to him day and night? Will he delay long over them? I tell you, he will give justice to them speedily."

This is a wonderful, theologically rich conclusion to the parable. A woman who had been overlooked by virtually everyone was finally given her due by this judge, who was simply exasperated with her continual coming. The point Jesus was making is both powerful and precious. We are to understand that this widow's persistence wore down even a crooked and unrighteous judge. He contrasted that unjust judge with the infinitely just God who "will . . . give justice to his elect, who cry to him day and night."

This parable reminds us of Jesus' teaching in Matthew 7. Speaking to his disciples, Jesus said: "Ask, and it will be given to you; seek, and you will find; knock, and it will be opened to you. For everyone who asks receives, and the one who seeks finds, and to the one who knocks it will be opened. Or which one of you, if his son asks him for bread, will give him a stone? Or if he asks for a fish, will give him a serpent? If you then, who are evil, know how to give good gifts to your children, how much more will your Father who is in heaven give good things to those who ask him!" (vv. 7–11).

The contrast between the human father and the heavenly Father is so clearly understood in Matthew's passage and in the parable of the persistent widow. Our heavenly Father longs to give us all good things, and he is always faithful to his word. When he makes a promise, he keeps it. He always acts in a way that is completely consistent with his character and power. If even sinful human fathers know how to give good gifts to their children, how much more so will our heavenly

Father give good gifts to us? Jesus told us to ask and it will be given, to seek and we will find, to knock and it will be opened to us.

Several themes in this parable deserve our attention before we turn to the shocking question that Jesus asked his disciples immediately after he concluded the parable. First, we need to recognize the power of the powerless in the kingdom of God. This judge thought himself powerful. After all, it was he who held the judgeship, he to whom people turned when they sought justice, he who handed down decisions and settled disputes. The judge appeared to be the one with power—but he eventually yielded to the greater power of this widow's persistence.

The Bible is extremely direct about the importance of caring for vulnerable people, including widows. *Especially* widows. In Deuteronomy 27:19 Israel was warned, "'Cursed be anyone who perverts the justice due to the sojourner, the fatherless, and the widow.' And the people shall say, 'Amen.'" Care for the widow was to be extended not only by the law and human judges but by those who bore responsibility to see to it that widows had food. The children of Israel were told that when they reaped a harvest, if they forgot a sheaf in the field they were not to go back and get it. Instead, "it shall be for the sojourner, the fatherless, and the widow, that the LORD your God may bless you in all the work of your hands" (Deut. 24:19).

The same exhortation is extended to the church. The expectation is that the church as the body of Christ will pay particular care to those most vulnerable. The apostle James wrote, "Religion that is pure and undefiled before God the Father is this: to visit orphans and widows in their affliction, and to keep oneself unstained from the world" (James 1:27). Jesus lifted up a widow who gave all she had (even though it was a small amount of money) as an example of faith and obedience to God. Again and again the Bible tells the people of God to look for greatness in the most unlikely of places and unlikely of persons. So perhaps it should come as no surprise that Jesus valorized a widow in this parable, giving her heroic status in the kingdom in the sense that she serves as a model to teach all disciples to pray without losing heart.

Second, we must work at a comprehensively biblical understanding of prayer. Jesus was concerned that his disciples ought always to pray and not lose heart—revealing yet again that Jesus understands us better than we understand ourselves. Jesus, as John tells us, knows what is inside of man. He knows our hearts and minds. He knows the temptation to doubt. He knows the temptation to crumble under the weight of fatigue and frustration. He knows what it means for us to lose heart. Understanding us better than we understand ourselves, he told the disciples this parable in order that they would not lose heart but would continue to pray faithfully, even when results seem far away.

When Jesus taught his disciples to pray in what we know as the Lord's Prayer, he gave them a pattern for prayer that takes the form of just a few words: "Our Father in heaven, hallowed be your name. Your kingdom come, your will be done, on earth as it is in heaven. Give us this day our daily bread, and forgive us our debts, as we also have forgiven our debtors. And lead us not into temptation, but deliver us from evil" (Matt. 6:9–13). The concerns in this prayer are practical—food, forgiveness, spiritual protection—and Jesus has authorized us to bring these concerns before the Lord in prayer. To pray without losing heart means that we are to pray according to his own instruction and his own example. We are not to lose heart, because God is never unfaithful. We are not to lose heart, not because our prayers follow any kind of magical formula, but precisely because God hears the prayers of his own and he will always vindicate his own people.

The temptation to lose heart comes because prayers are not always answered on our timetable or in the way we would design. But trusting God means trusting that he will give justice to his elect, that he will give us all we need. Our task in light of that reality is never to lose heart and, following the example of this persistent widow, to come before God regularly, making our needs and the cries of our heart known. God, unlike the unjust judge in this parable who simply relents to the widow's persistent pressure, is the gracious and merciful God who knows us better than we know ourselves and takes care of us beyond our expectations and imaginations.

But the astounding turn in this passage came when Jesus asked the question that grabs with force and will not let us go: "Nevertheless, when the Son of Man comes, will he find faith on earth?"

This is one of Scripture's verses that has framed my Christian imagination for all my adult life and has prompted some of the deepest and most urgent thinking and praying and working of my life in ministry. As I continue my discipline of constantly rereading the Scriptures, this passage in which the Son of God incarnate asks if, upon his return, he will find faith on earth, never fails to stop me in my tracks.

What are we to do with such a question? Is it doubtful that when the Son of Man comes, he will find faith—and the faithful—on earth? Is it possible that the Christian faith will be extinguished, and the Christian church would be wiped from the face of the earth? Is it conceivable that Christ would return and find his church fundamentally unfaithful, the gospel unpreached, the faith unconfessed?

It is *inconceivable* that when the Son of Man comes, he will find no faith on the earth. Jesus has told us that himself. Just remember what Jesus said as he declared the existence of the church: "On this rock I will build my church, and the gates of hell shall not prevail against it" (Matt. 16:18). Indeed, the gates of hell—the power of death—shall not prevail against the church. No human power will be able to extinguish the church and silence the gospel. No earthly power will be able to deny the Son of Man the faith on earth that he deserves to find upon his coming.

But Jesus did ask the question, and it should shock us. What could Jesus have been asking here and what are we to learn from it?

Jesus' question points to the necessity of the church's persistence in faith and faithfulness until he comes. The Christian church is called to preach the gospel, to contend for the faith, to hold to the doctrine, to wait in expectation, to worship with boldness, to share the gospel with all the nations, making disciples until Jesus comes. No earthly power can win final victory over the church, though persecution and martyrdom have been the lot of so many Christians throughout the centuries. When Jesus said that the gates of hell would not prevail against the church, he was giving us assurance. When Jesus asked if when the Son of Man comes he will find faith on the earth, he was challenging us to faithfulness.

Jesus' question is shocking and humbling, but we can see throughout history how church has been both faithful and faithless. We understand that there has been, from the beginning, a temptation to compromise biblical doctrine, to lose our grasp of the saving gospel of Christ, to turn to some other gospel and to preach some other message. Under today's secular conditions, the church is constantly put under pressure to compromise various elements of biblical truth and principles of morality.

In all too many places we see the results of a liberalized theology and a secularized Christianity. We see empty cathedrals and cultures growing increasingly hostile to Christianity. But Jesus has preserved his church, and the gates of hell shall not prevail. When the Son of Man comes, he will find faith on earth because it is he who gives his church faith and it is he who holds his church in the faith.

I can only imagine that when Jesus asked this question, the disciples were startled and anxious. No doubt, he got their attention. With equal force, he gets our attention now. It is the Christian task in every generation to "contend for the faith that was once for all delivered to the saints" (Jude v. 3). It is the responsibility of every generation of Christians to pass on the faith intact, in truth, in power, and in faithfulness. In every generation until Jesus comes it is our responsibility to follow the example of all those faithful Christians who've come before us, and even the example of this persistent widow, to make certain that when the Son of Man comes, he will find faith on earth.

# 1 0

# The Exalted Humbled and the Humble Exalted

## THE PARABLE OF THE PHARISEE AND THE TAX COLLECTOR

But now the righteousness of God has been manifested apart from the Law, although the Law and the Prophets bear witness to it—the righteousness of God through faith in Jesus Christ for all who believe. For there is no distinction: for all have sinned and fall short of the glory of God, and are justified by his grace as a gift, through the redemption that is in Christ Jesus, whom God put forward as a propitiation by his blood, to be received by faith. This was to show God's righteousness, because in his divine forbearance he had passed over former sins. It was to show his righteousness at the present time, so that he might be just and the justifier of the one who has faith in Jesus.

—ROMANS 3:21-26

Therefore, since we have been justified by faith, we
have peace with God through our Lord Jesus Christ.

—ROMANS 5:1

He also told this parable to some who trusted in themselves
that they were righteous, and treated others with contempt:
"Two men went up into the temple to pray, one a Pharisee and
the other a tax collector. The Pharisee, standing by himself,
prayed thus: 'God, I thank you that I am not like other men,
extortioners, unjust, adulterers, or even like this tax collector.
I fast twice a week; I give tithes of all that I get.' But the tax
collector, standing far off, would not even lift up his eyes to
heaven, but beat his breast, saying, 'God, be merciful to me,
a sinner!' I tell you, this man went down to his house justified,
rather than the other. For everyone who exalts himself will be
humbled, but the one who humbles himself will be exalted."
(Luke 18:9–14)

When Jesus told the parable of the persistent widow, he created
a picture that would have surprised the disciples. But the next
parable Jesus shared would have had a familiar ring, with two characters who would have been immediately understandable to the disciples:
the Pharisee and the tax collector. Both were fixtures in the imagination of those who heard Jesus tell this parable. The Pharisees were
ubiquitous in Jerusalem, loud in their piety and ostentatious in their
self-righteousness. They lived to be seen. The tax collectors, on the
other hand, were a part of the underclass. Indeed, they epitomized
complicity with Rome, criminality, and unrighteousness. As you

might expect, there is far more to this parable than meets the eye. But it begins with a comment about those to whom Jesus spoke it.

We learn that Jesus told this parable "to some who trusted in themselves that they were righteous, and treated others with contempt." Those two descriptors go together. Self-righteousness is one of the primal sins identified in Scripture. It is rooted in an illusion and an arrogance that simply cannot be hidden. It is true that men and women live lives of variable righteousness in terms of personal morality. The Bible is clear about that. Christians are called to obedience to God's Word and to holiness. We are called to avoid sin and unrighteousness. But even as we are called to live holy lives, we recognize that there is absolutely no righteousness in us. The Bible's indictment of our unrighteousness is comprehensive. Indeed, the prophet Isaiah declared that our righteousness is as filthy rags (64:6). There is no goodness in us. In the words of the *Book of Common Prayer*, "There is no health in us."

Understood in this context, Jesus told this dramatic parable to puncture the illusion of self-righteousness among those who heard him.

Jesus explained that two men went up to pray. While this concept of going *up* to pray might be surprising to many readers, the temple sat upon a mount in Jerusalem, which meant that people going to the temple went, in physical terms, up in order to pray. In first-century Judaism, the expression "going up" denoted a righteous act of holiness, reverence, and worship. The righteous Jews were invited to make their way up to the temple in order to worship God through sacrifice and prayer. There was nothing unusual about this Pharisee making his way up to the temple to pray. But it would have been more than a little shocking that the tax collector did the same.

In the Judaism of the day the tax collector would almost assuredly have been denied access to a synagogue, which had the right to restrict its own membership. But by God's law, the temple was a place for Israel to assemble, and this man, though a tax collector, could have made his way into the court of Israel. But it would have been a shockingly audacious act in the minds of the Pharisees. The crowd who heard Jesus speak this parable would have recoiled in indignation.

But what about the Pharisee? From the earliest days of my Christian experience, Bible teachers trained me to hear the word *Pharisee* with judgment. Most Christians have the same response. And yet, there is more to the Pharisees than that quick judgment. The Pharisees were truly seeking to be righteous and to show their righteousness before others. The Pharisees' central problem is that their righteousness was a *self-righteousness*, not a righteousness that comes from God. Pharisees were evidently traumatized by the understanding that they could not demonstrate righteousness, even to themselves, merely by obedience to the law. The Pharisees kept adding to the law in order to try to convince themselves that they had actually achieved a form of righteousness that would be acceptable to God. In Matthew 6, Jesus warned the disciples not to pray as the Pharisees prayed, with their ostentatious piety. Throughout Scripture the Pharisees are shown to commit the fatal error of trusting in their own righteousness. They were right to seek after righteousness, but they were wrong to think they had found it in themselves.

The point, however, is that those who heard Jesus tell this parable would not have been offended by the idea of the Pharisee going up to the temple to pray. It's what Pharisees did, and they were often held in admiration by temple authorities. They represented the morally upright, scrupulous, and ostentatiously pious. The audience who heard this parable would have assumed that the temple was right where the Pharisee belonged.

The tax collector, however, presented a real problem for Jesus' audience. The temple represented the apex of holiness—after all,

God's presence filled the temple. This would be the last place a first-century Jew would expect to find a tax collector. The tax collectors lived traitorous lives, selling out their nation to the Roman Empire by exacting pagan tolls and taxes on the people. They were opportunistic men who did business with idolaters and enforced Roman oppression. They lined their pockets with the wealth of their own neighbors by predatory action. In the minds of those hearing this parable, the tax collector should have had no place in the temple of God.

In short, in starting the parable by saying that two men went up to the temple to pray, one a Pharisee and the other a tax collector, Jesus surely grabbed the attention of his audience, as he has ours.

## Two Men at Prayer

Jesus described the prayers of these two men, and significantly, he told us something of their posture as well. In both the prayers and the postures we see a contrast between self-righteousness and a heart that comes before God knowing that it bears no righteousness at all. The prayer offered by the Pharisee is almost like a set piece—a caricature of what we would expect a self-righteous person to pray. And yet, this prayer is entirely believable coming from the lips of a first-century Pharisee. We are told that the Pharisee stood by himself. His posture was one of self-assurance: he stood apart, seeing the masses as unworthy of being in his presence. "God, I thank you that I am not like other men, extortioners, unjust, adulterers, or even like this tax collector. I fast twice a week; I give tithes of all that I get."

The most important thing to recognize about the Pharisee's prayer is that it is essentially self-referential. Even before speaking to God about himself, he thanked God that he was not like the others he observed—the great mass of Jewish men worshiping alongside him and especially the tax collector, whom he had noticed. Both the Pharisee and the tax collector were standing apart from the larger group of worshipers, but for two diametrically opposed reasons. The Pharisee considered himself superior to others, while the tax collector knew himself to be inferior.

The Pharisee was in a rush to assure himself that he was not like other men, perhaps even those he saw in the room. He was not an extortioner, he was not unjust by his self-evaluation, he was not an adulterer, and he was certainly not a tax collector. This tells us something about the danger of seeing our spiritual condition in contrast with others. Comparison simply will not work. There is no exercise in self-delusion more classic than this, to assure ourselves of our own goodness and righteousness precisely because we are not guilty of committing specific sins of which others are guilty. What's missing from the picture is the inherent sinfulness of every single one of us, including the sin of self-righteousness on the part of the self-righteous.

We also need to note that after contrasting himself with others, the Pharisee continued to read his résumé to God. He offered his credentials, stating, "I fast twice a week; I give tithes of all that I get." Note that this pattern of fasting and tithing is actually beyond the requirements of the law. They knew that their observance of the law brought them no assurance of righteousness, so they added to the law. We can understand this kind of pernicious logic. In some sense, the self-righteous know they are not righteous. There's a fundamental, constant insecurity in trying to assure ourselves of our own righteousness. Comparison with others is just the first step in trying to compensate for that insecurity, but it doesn't last. This man quickly moved on to bragging about his piety.

The Pharisee in this parable represents exactly what is wrong with false religion and false worship. It is about ourselves, rather than about God. There is no declaration in the Pharisee's prayer of the holiness and righteousness of God. There is no confession of sin. It is all about the Pharisee, from beginning to end. His purpose in worship is to convince God of his superiority as compared to others.

Meanwhile, the tax collector was praying at the same time as the Pharisee, standing far off by himself. His posture was of one who knew himself to be unworthy of worship, but he was drawn by the compulsion to find God's mercy. While the Pharisee stood proudly, the tax collector was unwilling even to lift up his eyes to heaven, opting instead to beat his breast, a near universal sign of self-abnegation and humiliation. To bring our fist to our chest with bowed head and lowered face is to demonstrate grief and brokenness. That is all this man knew to do. His prayer was short, and it had nothing to do with others in the temple. He simply cried out, "God, be merciful to me a sinner!" It is an exceedingly short prayer. It reminds me of the thief on the cross who, in a moment of agony as time was running out, simply turned to Jesus and said, "Jesus, remember me when you come into your kingdom" (Luke 23:42). Sometimes the shortest prayer is the sincerest prayer. Sometimes we simply have no words adequate to express our grief and remorse, our brokenheartedness and our repentance.

Christians should be encouraged by Paul's message to the Romans about how the Holy Spirit helps us, even articulating our prayers when we are unable to find the words. Paul wrote, "Likewise, the Spirit helps us in our weakness. For we do not know what to pray for as we ought, but the Spirit himself intercedes for us with groanings too deep for words. And he who searches hearts knows what is the mind of the Spirit, because the Spirit intercedes for the saints according to the will of God" (Rom. 8:26–27).

Jesus' point is clear. The brief, sincere prayer of the tax collector is the prayer of authentic repentance. He prayed for God's mercy. Christians must keep in mind that the word *mercy* does not just mean kindness. It means grace extended to those who have no claim upon it. Mercy as extended by a parent, a ruler, or a judge is understood to be undeserved. That's what makes mercy. And this is infinitely true when we speak of the mercy of God. This tax collector simply asked God to be merciful upon him, a sinner. That one word, "sinner," encapsulated everything he knew to say about himself and everything he needed to say about himself.

When I give my testimony of coming to faith in Christ, I often tell people that I had known even as a young child that I sinned. That was painfully obvious. But what was essential for my salvation was the knowledge of myself not only as one who sinned but as a *sinner*. In other words, the Holy Spirit brought me to understand that it was not merely the case that I sinned against God, but that in my heart I was a sinner. The problem was not just what I did, but who I was. Only then did I know to turn to Christ and seize him, believing in him and repenting of my sins. Only then did I become a Christian.

The knowledge of ourselves as sinners is essential. It's not just the fact that every one of us has sinned, but that every one of us is a sinner. The tax collector's confession is an encapsulation of the profound reality that his sin pervaded everything about him. This is the meaning of total depravity. The doctrine of total depravity does not mean that every one of us does as much evil as we are capable of, nor does it mean that everything we do is inherently sinful. What it does mean is that every single dimension of our being and every single act and thought of our experience is corrupted by sin. The reason for this is simple: it is a sinner doing the thinking and the doing. Furthermore, it is not just our will that is corrupted but our body, heart, and soul.

Most people who come to a saving knowledge of Christ don't

possess a detailed knowledge of the doctrine of sin or the reality of total depravity. But they do know that they are sinners in need of a savior. That knowledge is demonstrated in the prayer of this tax collector.

Significantly, as anyone who's familiar with the Old Testament should know, God would not hear the prayer of the Pharisee, but he would hear the prayer of the tax collector. Israel was warned repeatedly not to offer empty prayers devoid of contrition. Just as there were sacrifices that put a stench in God's nostrils, so also there were prayers that offended God's character. One prayer we can be assured God will always hear is the prayer of confession in response to the gospel.

Jesus made this point emphatically clear in the climactic conclusion of the parable—a conclusion that goes much further than most Christians seem to recognize: "I tell you, this man went down to his house justified, rather than the other. For everyone who exalts himself will be humbled, but the one who humbles himself will be exalted."

Many would assume that Jesus would end the parable by telling us that both men went home justified. The conventional theology of the day would have said that the Pharisee belonged in the temple and that he would certainly find justification in the judgment of God. But Jesus eliminated this possibility and condemned the Pharisee as unjustified. His sins remained upon him. He claimed a self-righteousness, and that self-righteousness would on the day of judgment be revealed as an anti-righteousness, no righteousness at all. Jesus declared that only one man went home justified and it wasn't the Pharisee. It was the tax collector. Speaking to those who trusted in themselves that they were righteous and treated others with contempt, Jesus went so far as to tell them not only that they were not truly righteous but that the very people they held in contempt might well show up in the kingdom of God as justified because, unlike the Pharisee, they came to a knowledge of their sin and cried out to God for mercy.

# The False Gospel of Moralism

Moralism reigns as the most dangerous of all false gospels. The tendency to moralize exists because the Bible contains so much moral teaching in both the Old and New Testaments. There is moral content to the revelation of God, coming in the form of laws and statutes and commands. Christ himself declared in the Sermon on the Mount that he had not come to abolish the Law and the Prophets but to fulfill them: "Not the smallest letter or stroke shall pass from the Law until all is accomplished" (Matt. 5:18 NASB95). Further, whenever he used the phrase "You have heard" in the Sermon on the Mount, what followed was not moral revisionism that lowered the moral expectation, but rather a gospel intensification of the morality that God expects. For example:

> "You have heard that the ancients were told, 'YOU SHALL NOT COMMIT MURDER' and 'Whoever commits murder shall be liable to the court.' But I say to you that everyone who is angry with his brother shall be guilty before the court." . . . Or, "You have heard that it was said, 'YOU SHALL NOT COMMIT ADULTERY'; but I say to you that everyone who looks at a woman with lust for her has already committed adultery with her in his heart."
>
> (MATT. 5: 21–22; 27–28 NASB95)

To be clear: the problem is not morality, but *moralism*. Moralism says, whether explicitly or implicitly, that God expects us to *behave*. But what God expects of us is to *believe* and trust in Christ. There will be plenty of well-behaved people in hell. The false gospel of moralism tells people that salvation comes by behaving, and they convince themselves that they can trust in their behavior. Moralism is a false gospel not only because it takes morality out of its gospel context in Scripture but because it leads us to the self-delusion of believing ourselves to be moral and righteous.

The false gospel of moralism works in several insidious ways. It makes us feel better about ourselves and more comfortable in our own skin. We look at our own moral behavior (or at least what we perceive to be our moral behavior) and hold it up as a confirmation of our spiritual status. Like the Pharisee, this comes most naturally to us when there are others to whom we can compare ourselves. There is no greater confirmation of moralism than a feeling of our own moral superiority. In the same sense, moralism gives us an opportunity to keep score, and human beings are *very* good at keeping score, in moral standards of our own devising. We'll give ourselves a far higher score than we will give others.

Christians are called to holiness, according to the law of Christ. Even as moralism is a false gospel, so is antinomianism (literally, anti-law or lawlessness), the false message that all that is required for salvation is intellectual assent to the facts of the gospel. Intellectual assent to the truth of the gospel is necessary, but the New Testament makes clear that obedience to Christ is also necessary. The key distinction is that it is our salvation that produces the obedience, not our obedience that produces the salvation. The Bible reveals salvation by grace alone through faith alone in Christ alone. There is no grace if grace is not alone in this sense.

The temptation to moralize this parable reveals just how easy it is to fall into the false gospel of moralism. If we're not careful, we can end up reading the parable of the Pharisee and the tax collector *as Pharisees*. Even Christians who know the gospel of Jesus Christ are tempted to think of themselves as morally superior to the Pharisee precisely because they would never articulate a prayer like his. Moralism is so seductive that it can convince us that we're morally superior because we hold to a morally superior form of moralism. This parable confronts us with the danger of descending into an endless cycle of self-justification and self-deception.

The subtlety of moralism shows itself when we allow comparison to others to provide the framework for understanding our spiritual condition. Christians need to recognize that we are always fighting against an inner Pharisee. That inner Pharisee is always there, tempting us, even when reading a parable like this, to feel ourselves superior to those who are described. But salvation comes only to the one who comes to genuine repentance as exemplified here by the tax collector, who skipped self-justifying comparisons to others in the room and recognized himself as a sinner before God.

Jesus concluded his parable with a sober warning against self-exaltation that serves as a fitting interpretive principle for the parable he had just told: "Everyone who exalts himself will be humbled, but the one who humbles himself will be exalted." The Pharisee exalted himself, but he will be humbled. The tax collector humbled himself, but he will be exalted. This reversal of our expectations reveals why we must always have an eschatological frame of reference. Righteousness and unrighteousness will only finally and definitively be revealed on the Day of the Lord, the great Day of Judgment. On that day those who have exalted themselves will be humbled and those who have humbled themselves in Christ will be exalted. Until then, looks can be deceiving.

## A Warning About Worship

This parable also reveals the danger of worship that does not please God. We have seen the Pharisee's proud posture and self-aggrandizing prayer in the temple. Now consider the experience of Isaiah during his calling as a prophet in Isaiah 6. While in the temple, Isaiah "saw the Lord sitting upon a throne, high and lifted up; and the train of his robe filled the temple" (v. 1). He witnessed the overwhelming power of the six-winged seraphim who called to one another a threefold declaration of God's holiness: "Holy, holy, holy is the LORD of hosts; the whole earth is full of his glory!" (v. 3). But then we are told what followed that declaration of God's threefold holiness. The temple filled with smoke. And upon hearing the earth-shaking sound of God's voice calling him, Isaiah cried out, "Woe is me! For I am lost; for I am a man of unclean lips, and I dwell in the midst of a people of unclean lips; for my eyes have seen the King, the LORD of hosts!" (v. 5).

The contrast here is astounding. Isaiah and the Pharisee were both in the temple, but Isaiah saw a vision of the Lord high and lifted up. Isaiah heard the declaration that God is holy, holy, holy, the thrice-holy God. Isaiah's response to the infinite holiness of God was to acknowledge his own sinfulness in no uncertain terms: "Woe is me! For I am lost; for I am a man of unclean lips, and I dwell in the midst of a people of unclean lips." How did Isaiah know this? Because his "eyes have seen the King, the LORD of hosts!" Isaiah was not in the temple in order to seek self-knowledge. He was in the temple to worship God. And when he saw the vision of God's perfect holiness, his only response was to understand and confess his own sinfulness. In contrast, the Pharisee looked to himself, basically worshiped himself, absolved himself of guilt, and went home unjustified.

Considering these two examples together clarifies the danger of false worship. The Pharisee undoubtedly went home convinced that he had worshiped. But he was fundamentally unchanged. Furthermore, his worship was self-worship disguised as the worship of God.

Self-worship is perhaps the most deceitful of all idolatries. This parable indicts all forms of false worship, including the sheer superficiality of what passes for worship in so many churches. There is no sense of the profound holiness of God. There is no sense of the weight and majesty of God's glory, no declaration of the infinite greatness of God as our Lord and King. There is no pattern of acknowledgment of the triune God as Father, Son, and Holy Spirit, and there is no sense of the magnificent majesty of God. So much of what is called worship in evangelical circles actually represents a horizontalization of what should be most profoundly vertical. Our worship should be vertical, directed to our Father in heaven. Worship is not a celebration of fellowship, a therapeutic confirmation of self-knowledge, or a form of entertainment.

But we must again remind ourselves to beware of believing that in avoiding the Pharisee's example we have achieved anything. Merely avoiding his example does not lead to salvation. We have to follow the humble example of the tax collector.

## The Centrality of Justification

Pay close attention to how Jesus highlighted the centrality of justification to our salvation. He told us that the tax collector, not the Pharisee, went home justified. Martin Luther, the great reformer of the sixteenth century, was exactly right when he described justification as *articulus stantis et cadentis ecclesiae*—the article by which the church stands and falls. This is where the gospel is made most clear and where the purity of the gospel is most likely to become compromised. The New Testament teaches that Christ died for our justification. In Romans 3, Paul said that on the cross, God put Christ forth as a propitiation by his blood, to be received by faith. Paul then wrote, "This was to show God's righteousness, because in his divine forbearance he had passed over former sins. It was to show his righteousness at the present time, so that he might be just and the justifier of the one who has faith in Jesus" (vv. 25–26). In this amazing passage Paul explained that the atonement accomplished by the Lord Jesus Christ was a propitiation whereby God's disposition toward sinners was changed. Those sinners who come to faith in the Lord Jesus Christ are justified even as God remains just, because he both *required* and *provided* the necessary penalty for sin.

But where is the righteousness? Justification explains that those who are justified by Christ bear Christ's own righteousness. If we are in Christ, our sin is imputed to Jesus on the cross, and his righteousness is imputed to us. Therefore, what God sees when he looks to those who are in Christ is the imputed righteousness of his Son. The righteousness of Christ is the only grounds for our justification, and we receive it only by faith. This faith is a trusting, believing acknowledgment that there is no righteousness in us, but that Christ is our righteousness.

Until Jesus comes, justification by faith alone will remain the article by which the church stands or falls. In this parable, we see this truth affirmed by the Lord Jesus Christ himself.

# 11

# The Shrewd Sons of This Age

## THE PARABLE OF THE DISHONEST MANAGER

> He frustrates the devices of the crafty, so that their hands achieve no success. He catches the wise in their own craftiness, and the schemes of the wily are brought to a quick end. They meet with darkness in the daytime and grope at noonday as in the night.
>
> —JOB 5:12–14

> "Do not lay up for yourselves treasures on earth, where moth and rust destroy and where thieves break in and steal, but lay up for yourselves treasures in heaven, where neither moth nor rust destroys and where thieves do not break in and steal. For where your treasure is, there your heart will be also. . . . No one can serve two masters, for either he will hate the one and love the other, or he will be devoted to the one and despise the other. You cannot serve God and money."
>
> —MATTHEW 6:19–21, 24

Now He was also saying to the disciples, "There was a rich man who had a manager, and this manager was reported to him as squandering his possessions. And he called him and said to him, 'What is this I hear about you? Give an accounting of your management, for you can no longer be manager.' The manager said to himself, 'What shall I do, since my master is taking the management away from me? I am not strong enough to dig; I am ashamed to beg. I know what I shall do, so that when I am removed from the management people will welcome me into their homes.' And he summoned each one of his master's debtors, and he began saying to the first, 'How much do you owe my master?' And he said, 'A hundred measures of oil.' And he said to him, 'Take your bill, and sit down quickly and write fifty.' Then he said to another, 'And how much do you owe?' And he said, 'A hundred measures of wheat.' He said to him, 'Take your bill, and write eighty.' And his master praised the unrighteous manager because he had acted shrewdly; for the sons of this age are more shrewd in relation to their own kind than the sons of light. And I say to you, make friends for yourselves by means of the wealth of unrighteousness, so that when it fails, they will receive you into the eternal dwellings." (Luke 16:1–9 NASB95)

The parables always surprise us, but in this case the parable is a surprise from beginning to end. It is such a perplexing story that many Christians have missed the main point Jesus was making, and instead see it as a disconcerting affirmation of a crook at work.

Of course, the parable means nothing of the sort. Jesus told this story as a warning against trust in riches, but he had other lessons for the disciples to learn as well. In Luke 16:1 we are told that Jesus shared this parable privately with the disciples, not with the world at large. This parable is specifically for us, the church, and we had better pay close attention to it. Not that there is any danger we could forget this parable.

The story is straightforward enough in its narrative form, but shockingly, the central character is a crook, described as both dishonest and shrewd. As we will see, sometimes it's hard to tell the difference between dishonesty and shrewdness.

The story begins with a rich man who had heard that the manager he had made responsible for administering his affairs was actually wasting his wealth. Understandably, he confronted the manager, asking, "What is this I hear about you?" The rich man's question was really just a precursor to firing the manager: "Give an accounting of your management, for you can no longer be manager." The setup is simple enough. The manager's malfeasance was so obvious and extensive that the rich man fired him outright.

But then we discover that the fired manager is the central character of Jesus' parable, not the wealthy man. In a soliloquy, the manager said to himself, "What shall I do, since my master is taking the management away from me? I am not strong enough to dig; I am ashamed to beg." Having lost a comfortable position that had brought him income and status, the manager would soon be thrown out on the street.

The man did have some self-knowledge. He was honest enough to recognize that he had neither the strength for manual labor nor the humility to be financially dependent upon others. But he did have a certain amount of financial skill, so he decided that he would apply that in a way that would secure for him friends, and perhaps future employment. He came to the conclusion that he would ingratiate himself by financial dealings with people who "will welcome me into their homes."

His crooked plot was both sophisticated and clever. He decided to bring in his master's most important clients and debtors and cut them individual deals. To the first debtor, who owed the master a hundred measures of oil, the manager offered a 50 percent discount: "Take your bill, and sit down quickly and write fifty." The manager called in another debtor to his master and asked what he owed. When the man responded that he owed a hundred measures of wheat, once again the manager gave him a discount: "Take your bill, and write eighty." The manager was evidently such a good student of human character that he could buy this man off with a much less significant discount than the first. In any event, what we see here is not only mismanagement and malfeasance but criminal activity. The manager was betraying the financial trust that had been given to him by the man of wealth. His responsibility was to steward and build the man's wealth, but he was undermining it, to his own advantage.

The disgraced manager had just bought two friends. Both of them came at quite a price, but it was not the manager himself who paid the price, but his former master, the rich man.

If the parable was not sufficiently shocking to this point, it became even more surprising when the master returned—and actually commended the dishonest manager for his shrewdness!

This was a twist in the tale no one could have expected. Not only had Jesus placed a criminal at the center of the story as its most important character, but this character's criminal activity was transformed into a way of ingratiating himself with the very man whose financial interests he had been subverting. The rich man returned and was so impressed with the plan put into effect by this manager that he decided he could not be without him. Anyone who could pull off this kind of scheme was simply too talented and wily to be trusted to work for anyone else. This, reasoned the rich man, is the kind of talent you have to keep close at hand.

In recap, a rich man found out that his administrator was guilty of mismanagement, so he fired him. As Jesus made clear, the manager was too weak to dig and too proud to beg and he was facing the reality of living on the streets. So he decided to put into effect a scheme whereby he would offer his master's clients an extremely significant discount in order to make friends with them. He acted in a way that not only continued his mismanagement but turned it into utter criminality. But when the rich man discovered the scheme, he decided that this manager was too shrewd to let go.

Speaking to the disciples, Jesus then said: "For the sons of this age are more shrewd in relation to their own kind than the sons of light."

Now, what are we to do with this parable? First, we ought to take note of some easy-to-miss details. First, Jesus simply referred to the man of wealth as "a rich man." That description is not as morally neutral as it may appear. Whenever Jesus mentioned a rich man in the context of a parable, as he would again in the parable of the rich man and Lazarus that follows, the rich man was simply assumed to be someone who trusted in riches and may well have obtained his wealth by suspicious means. When Jesus began a parable by saying, "There was a rich man," we should assume we're being introduced to someone of questionable character.

The next thing we need to note is that the rich man didn't fire the manager immediately, but rather announced his imminent firing. This is what gave the man the opportunity to call in the debtors and offer them the discount. The story would have been very different had the man been sent out of his office immediately, with no opportunity for continued involvement in his master's affairs. Also note that there were others complicit in his crime, including those who knew full well that they owed the rich man a hundred measures of oil and a hundred measures of wheat, respectively. And yet they were quite eager to take the discount and consider it good luck and gain.

Of course, not many wealthy individuals would respond to a crooked employee in the way described in this parable. But as we know, a key feature of a parable is its ability to get our attention by subverting our expectations. But now that the parable has our attention, what exactly are we to understand from this story? Are we being told to go and follow the example of a dishonest employee who turns out to be a crook? Well, in one sense, yes. But the context is all-important.

This brings us back to those two descriptors: shrewd and unrighteous ("dishonest" in the ESV). Jesus described the manager in this parable as "unrighteous," while the rich man commended the man because he had acted "shrewdly." There's a vast difference between unrighteousness or dishonesty and shrewdness, though shrewdness can lead to dishonesty and may offer cover for a host of sins. But while dishonesty is directly condemned in Scripture as a sin, shrewdness is not necessarily a sin.

Examples of shrewdness in crime are as famous as some of the headline crime stories of recent years. In 2008 headlines all over the world reported the arrest of Bernie Madoff, who had stood as a paragon of Wall Street, at one time running the sixth-largest fund of S&P 500 stocks. Madoff turned out to be running a vast Ponzi scheme. He opened a penny stock brokerage in 1960, and then quickly began moving upscale in investments and in clientele. After his arrest, his clients were so shocked to learn that Madoff was a crook, they refused to believe it. Only with the collapse of the fund did many investors come to understand that they'd been scammed by one of the slickest investor criminals in history. No one yet knows exactly when Madoff's investment scheme shifted into sheer criminality. And yet, at one point upward of $65 billion was missing from client accounts when the scam collapsed.

Something about human nature is revealed in the fact that Bernie Madoff got most of his big client investors by acting as if they were not worthy of his attention. The essence of his salesmanship was that people connived and begged in order to get Madoff to accept their investment and bring them into the fund. The very idea of a "con" is a confidence game, and Bernie Madoff was a man who inspired so much confidence that people gave him billions of dollars and begged him to take more.

Of course, Madoff's tale came to a bitter end when he died in prison after being sentenced to 150 years behind bars. The fall of the house of Madoff was Shakespearean in its scale, with his two sons dying shortly after their father's crime had been exposed, one of cancer and the other by his own hand.

We refer to Bernie Madoff's scheme as a "Ponzi" because the entire scam is often identified with the man who's gone down in history as Charles Ponzi. Actually his name was Carlo Pietro Giovanni Guglielmo Tebaldo Ponzi. He came to the United States in the late nineteenth century and soon began building his own scheme based upon taking advantage of exchange rates by arbitrage. He promised investors a 50 percent profit in forty-five days or 100 percent profit in ninety days. There is no actual investment that could promise those kinds of returns, but human nature is demonstrated by how people wanted to give Ponzi that money in order that they might receive those incredible returns. By the time Ponzi's scheme failed and his business collapsed, he had lost about $20 million. At today's rates, that would be something like $250 million. All that pales, of course, when compared with Bernie Madoff's collapse, but Ponzi's scheme was infamous enough that an entire arena of crime was named for him.

In their own way, Bernie Madoff and Charles Ponzi serve as reminders that the dishonest manager in Jesus' parable has a lot of company.

Jesus used the term "shrewdness" to instruct his disciples about how they were to take advantage of opportunities for the sake of the kingdom of heaven. In one of the most amazing passages in the Gospel of Luke, Jesus instructed his disciples that "the sons of this age are more shrewd in relation to their own kind than the sons of light." This contrast between the sons of this age and the sons of light echoes the contrast between the children of light and the children of darkness that we've seen in other passages. This distinction between the children of light and the children of darkness is a reminder of how every single human being at every single moment belongs either to Christ or to the devil.

But Jesus' point was that the sons of darkness, "the sons of this age," are more shrewd in dealing with their generation than the sons of light. What does this mean?

In order to understand this, it is helpful to consider the essence of criminality. The essence of crime consists in the criminal seeing an opportunity and seizing it. That's exactly what this dishonest manager did. He saw the opportunity to ingratiate himself at his master's expense. He seized the opportunity and the plan worked. It worked so well that it impressed the man who had fired him, who then turned around and rehired him, realizing that he could not do without him.

Humans—even those who are not themselves criminals—seem to have a natural interest in criminality and the criminal mind. For some reason, we are captivated by watching a movie or reading a book in which a criminal makes a plan and carries it out. Of course, the very genre of the crime novel or movie is rooted in the moral reality that right and wrong actually exist. It is for this reason that the crime novel and similar kinds of literature and entertainment only make sense in a civilization shaped by the Christian worldview.

There can be no question about God's condemnation of criminality. Jesus was not valorizing a criminal in this parable; instead he was pointing to criminals with the knowledge that they look around them at all times seeking to find an opportunity. When they find that opportunity, they put their plan into action. Jesus appeared to be describing this skill as "shrewdness," and he was telling the disciples that his followers must be just as shrewd for the sake of the kingdom of heaven as criminals are for the kingdom of darkness. Like the criminal who sees the opportunity and understands it, who sizes up the situation and exploits it, Jesus said that those who are of the kingdom of heaven, the children of light, should be driven by the same intensity of purpose and imagination of opportunity as this criminal.

Interestingly, as Jesus concluded this parable he offered a point that summarized his purpose. In verse 9 Jesus told the disciples, "And I tell you, make friends for yourselves by means of the wealth of unrighteousness, so that when it fails, they will receive you into the eternal dwellings." It's a complicated sentence, but Jesus' point comes down to the lesson that the children of light are to be using money in this world in order to advance the kingdom of heaven. It is in that sense that the shrewdness of the crook becomes an example for Christians. This is certainly a motivation for Christian stewardship and generosity, because investment in the work of Christ will indeed bring heavenly results, a heavenly increase. At the end of the day, money will mean nothing in an eternal context, while the gain of the kingdom will mean everything eternally.

The children of light must be ready to put our wealth, our stewardship, our financial planning, and our investments in the service of the kingdom of heaven, and to understand how strategic investment in kingdom opportunities can be shrewdly identified and exploited.

Jesus went on to make an additional point about Christians and money, telling the disciples:

One who is faithful in a very little is also faithful in much, and one who is dishonest in a very little is also dishonest in much. If then you have not been faithful in the unrighteous wealth, who will entrust to you the true riches? And if you have not been faithful in that which is another's, who will give you that which is your own? No servant can serve two masters, for either he will hate the one and love the other, or he will be devoted to the one and despise the other. You cannot serve God and money. (Luke 16:10–13)

This is a lesson we can immediately understand. When it comes to the power of the kingdom, Jesus made clear that "the true riches" will be invested in those who faithfully serve the kingdom.

The warning that no one can serve two masters is also bracingly clear. We are called to serve the Lord Jesus Christ as our Master, and to be completely devoted to him. Love of money, as Paul told Timothy, "is a root of all kinds of evils," even leading some to wander away from the faith. Paul warned the church lest by the sin of materialism Christians be pierced "with many griefs" (1 Tim. 6:10 NIV).

So there we have it. We just encountered a parable of Jesus with a crook at the center, but a profound spiritual lesson for the church, illustrating the reality that stories of crime and punishment have always had the power to gain our attention. A crook is a crook is a crook. But the disciples of Jesus are told that they are to be just as shrewd as the sons of this world, but for the things of God and the kingdom of heaven. That's a lesson the disciples probably did not expect. If we're honest, neither did we.

# 12

# Miserly Fairness Versus Extravagant Grace

## THE LABORERS IN THE VINEYARD

But if it is by grace, it is no longer on the basis of works; otherwise grace would no longer be grace.

—ROMANS 11:6

For the grace of God has appeared, bringing salvation for all people, training us to renounce ungodliness and worldly passions, and to live self-controlled, upright, and godly lives in the present age, waiting for our blessed hope, the appearing of the glory of our great God and Savior Jesus Christ, who gave himself for us to redeem us all from lawlessness and to purify for himself a people for his own possession who are zealous for good works.

—TITUS 2:11-14

The grace of the Lord Jesus be with all. Amen.

—REVELATION 22:21

"For the kingdom of heaven is like a landowner who went out early in the morning to hire laborers for his vineyard. When he had agreed with the laborers for a denarius a day, he sent them into his vineyard. And he went out about the third hour and saw others standing idle in the market place; and to those he said, 'You also go into the vineyard, and whatever is right I will give you.' And so they went. Again he went out about the sixth hour and the ninth hour, and did the same thing. And about the eleventh hour he went out and found others standing around; and he said to them, 'Why have you been standing here idle all day long?' They said to him, 'Because no one hired us.' He said to them, 'You go into the vineyard too.'

"When evening came, the owner of the vineyard said to his foreman, 'Call the laborers and pay them their wages, beginning with the last group to the first.' When those hired about the eleventh hour came, each one received a denarius. When those hired first came, they thought they would receive more; but each of them also received a denarius. When they received it, they grumbled at the landowner, saying, 'These last men have worked only one hour, and you have made them equal to us who have borne the burden and the scorching heat of the day.' But he answered and said to one of them, 'Friend, I am doing you no wrong; did you not agree with me for a denarius? Take what is yours and go, but I wish to give to this last man the same as to you. Is it not lawful for me to do what I wish with what is my own? Or is your eye envious because

I am generous?' So the last shall be first, and the first last."
(Matt. 20:1–16 NASB95)

There's good evidence that the favorite hymn among Americans is John Newton's famous "Amazing Grace." Sadly, the song has slipped into the category of folk music in some circles, but we understand the reason why so many people are drawn to this hymn. In its utter simplicity, it presents the gospel of Jesus Christ. A secular age will try to disregard its gospel content, but there is no word so essential and unique to the Christian gospel as *grace*.

As we have seen, grace is at the center of the Christian gospel. We are saved by God's unmerited favor. As the apostle Paul wrote: "For by grace you have been saved through faith. And this is not your own doing; it is the gift of God, not a result of works, so that no one may boast" (Eph. 2:8–9). Paul could not have been clearer: we have nothing at all to contribute to our own salvation. From beginning to end, and at all points in between, it is grace, grace, and only God's grace. Paul explained that we are saved by grace alone through faith alone and that it is not in any sense our own doing. It is entirely and exclusively the gift of God, not the result of any good works. Therefore, there is no ground for our boasting. As Paul implied, if our righteousness had anything to do with our salvation, our boasting would be endless.

But even as we affirm the centrality of grace to the gospel of Jesus Christ, and even as Scripture instructs us that salvation comes by grace alone through faith alone in Christ alone, we also have to understand that human nature in its fallen state is entirely opposed to grace. Grace cuts against our pride and is contrary to the human impulse of fairness.

Actually, this is one of the inherent problems with an ethic of fairness. Fairness is not only deeply subjective but also endlessly frustrating. *Fair* works as a category for the supervision of children on a playground, but it is utterly inadequate when the issue at stake is sin. The last thing sinners should hope for is fairness, which would mean our eternal separation from God in hell. No, grace is the refutation of fairness, and that is entirely the point.

In the parable of the laborers in the vineyard, Jesus defined grace in a way that is both counterintuitive and frankly outrageous to human sensibilities. Jesus told the story of a landowner who went out in the early morning to hire laborers to work in his vineyard. Jesus began by explaining that the kingdom of heaven is like this landowner and his vineyard. What we are looking at here is another picture of the kingdom, where the laborers hired to work in the vineyard represent sinners saved by grace who are put to work on behalf of the kingdom of heaven. Jesus said that the man went out to hire laborers early in the morning, and at that early hour, 6:00 a.m., he made an arrangement with the laborers to work for a denarius a day, the expected rate. After hiring them, he sent them to work in his vineyard. So far, so good.

But the story continued. At the third hour (9:00 a.m.) the landowner saw other laborers standing idly in the marketplace. To them he said, "You also go into the vineyard, and whatever is right I will give you." We can imagine this situation, as day laborers are a part of just about every culture. However, modern readers might not know that day laborers were particularly vulnerable in the context of first-century Judaism. There were regulations that required employers to take care of their servants, who were considered part of the household. But day laborers were in an analogous situation to aliens and sojourners who had no citizenship. They belonged to no household that was responsible for their financial support and care. If they did not work, they did not eat, and it was as simple as that. These workers were at the bottom of the agricultural economy, and they were dependent upon landowners who would come to the marketplace to hire them early in the day so that they could earn a day's wages.

As the day unfolded in Jesus' parable, the man went to the marketplace several times to hire additional workers, saying simply, "Whatever is right I will give you." The workers (and anyone listening to the parable) would assume that those hired early in the morning would earn a full day's wage. Those hired later would earn a reasonable percentage. The first group was hired first thing in the morning, the second at about nine o'clock, the third at noon, the fourth at three, and the last at five, just an hour before the end of the workday (about 6:00 p.m. as the sun was setting).

Note that when the landowner went to the marketplace at the sixth hour, the ninth hour, and the eleventh hour, he saw the men standing and asked them, "Why have you been standing here idle all day long?" Their response to him was straightforward: "Because no one hired us." The landowner then hired them and sent them into the vineyard. Does this imply that the laborers who remained in the marketplace until hired later in the day were lazy or unwilling to work? No, there is no judgment made about them in this respect at all. To the contrary, they explained that they had not been working simply because they had not been hired. The point is that they were not called to work until the landowner issued the call, and upon that call they came.

The issue of payment is central to this story. We can understand exactly how the payment ought to have worked according to conventional wisdom. If those who worked all day expected a denarius, then those who worked three hours less could expect about 75 percent, those hired third about 50 percent, those hired at the ninth hour about 25 percent, and those hired at the last hour could expect to receive something like one-twelfth of the denarius. All this would be fair by human standards. Any wage is better than no wage, and the workers would have likely jumped at the opportunity regardless of the hour.

But, this being a parable, Jesus took the story in an unexpected direction, telling us that when the time came for payment, the master decided to first pay those hired last. Those who were hired first would be paid last. This order of events sets up the surprising moment when the first hired and the last paid discovered their wage. Jesus shared that those who were hired last came for their payment and "each one received a denarius." The story then fast-forwards to the payment of those who were hired first, and Jesus admitted straightforwardly, "They thought that they would receive more, but each of them also received a denarius."

Now we see the problem. If we are honest, this is at least mildly offensive to our sense of fairness. How is it that in any fair economic system someone working one hour can receive the same pay as someone who had worked twelve hours through the heat of the day? How is it that this could be fair according to any agreement that would be negotiated by labor and management? How does this fit our preconceptions of justice and equity? The reality is, the entire parable refutes our sense of fairness and equity.

Jesus explained that upon receiving their agreed-upon pay, those hired first "grumbled at the landowner, saying, 'These last men have worked only one hour, and you have made them equal to us who have borne the burden and the scorching heat of the day.'" They seem to have had a point. Any number of labor lawyers would be quite eager to take their case. If there were no court to which they could appeal, the court of public opinion would be likely to run against this master and his system of pay. We can understand the grumbling of the workers, for it seems that they had every reason to grumble.

But the landowner responded to one of those grumbling and said, "Friend, I am doing you no wrong; did you not agree with me for a denarius? Take what is yours and go, but I wish to give to this last man the same as to you." The landowner then asked an astounding question: "Is it not lawful for me to do what I wish with what is my own? Or is your eye envious because I am generous?"

The landowner was unmoved by the grumbling of those who complained against him. He simply reminded them that they had already agreed to the wage of a denarius and that after all, it was his right to pay those who came later in the day whatever he may choose. What are we to do with this landowner? How can we reason with such a person who thinks it's fair to give to those who came last as much as those who came first to the day's work? Remember that the master did not tell those hired after the first hour what they would be paid, only that he would give them "whatever is right." But was he right?

The landowner's response to the grumbling demonstrated his perspective. In blunt terms, he insisted that he was allowed to do what he chose with what belonged to him. If he chose to be generous, no one had the right to complain about his generosity. He was the lord of the vineyard, he would determine who was hired and who was paid, and he would decide what is fair. More than fair, he would decide what was *right* and *just*.

There is so much for us to see in this parable, which is indeed a picture of the kingdom of heaven. Jesus was explaining to his disciples that, like the laborers in the vineyard, we have no right to complain about God's gift of mercy and grace for anyone who believes. We come into the kingdom of God by the same call of the Holy Spirit. Like the laborers standing idly by in the marketplace, we are unable to do anything about our condition. Only the master of the vineyard can change our story. We come into the kingdom of heaven by his call and in his service.

And, this becomes the crucial point: every single one of us comes *by grace*. Understood rightly, this parable reminds us that grace is infinite. There was no obligation on the part of the master of the house to hire *any* of the laborers. Every single one of them was, rightly understood, hired by grace. Christians understand that grace is Christ, and that call is the call of the gospel—the call to believe and repent and be saved. We understand that there will be those who labor long in this life for the kingdom, and those who labor for a shorter time. But, judged against eternity, there is no difference between the first hour and the eleventh hour.

The extravagance of God's grace is made clear in this parable. None of us deserves in any sense to be hired. Salvation is entirely of grace, and grace is simply not fair. *Fair* would mean that no one is saved. Grace means that those whom God calls, he saves.

# The Grave Sin of Grumbling

There's another dimension to this story that concerns Jesus' use of one word in verse 11. We are told that those hired first and paid last "grumbled at the landowner." We tend to think of grumbling as something that, while wrong, is probably not so grave as other sins. Grumbling comes as something like second nature to us as human beings. We are not good at being quiet when we are unhappy. The Bible reveals grumbling to be one of the gravest of sins, indicative of far deeper problems than discontent.

We should think of the Israelites' experience in the book of Exodus. The Lord had led the children of Israel out of Egypt where they had been slaves to Pharaoh, he had brought them safely through the parted waters of the Red Sea and given them victory over Pharaoh's chariots, and he faithfully gave them evening meat and morning bread that made them full. In Exodus 16:8, Moses reminded the children of Israel of God's provision for them; nevertheless, they grumbled against the Lord, and Moses told them, "The LORD has heard your grumbling that you grumble against him. . . . Your grumbling is not against us but against the LORD."

To grumble is to complain about the goodness of God. In this sense, grumbling is the consummate act of ingratitude. It is also an incredible overreach that reeks of human arrogance. How dare we grumble against God, who has given us everything?

At various points in Israel's history, the temptation to grumble arose again and again. The children of Israel grumbled against Moses again when he sent out the spies to give a report on the land of promise. Many hundreds of years later, the apostle James warned the church against grumbling, lest we incur divine judgment: "Do not grumble against one another, brothers, so that you may not be judged; behold, the Judge is standing at the door" (James 5:9). Similarly, Paul exhorted Christians in Philippians 2:14 to "do all things without grumbling or disputing." In parallel to Israel's sin, grumbling in the church is, in effect, grumbling against the Lord Jesus Christ. How dare we?

In the parable of the laborers in the vineyard Jesus offered a graphic and unsettling picture of the glories of God's grace. Grace that is indeed greater than all our sin. How dare we grumble against grace? Jesus told this story in order to instruct and exhort the disciples, and this means all Christians throughout the ages. Every single one of us needs to hear this parable with full force, as we share the honor of working in the vineyard of the Lord.

# 13

## Well Done, Good and Faithful Servant

### THE PARABLE OF THE TALENTS

I have fought the good fight, I have finished the race, I have kept the faith. Henceforth there is laid up for me the crown of righteousness, which the Lord, the righteous judge, will award to me on that day, and not only to me but also to all who have loved his appearing.

—2 TIMOTHY 4:7–8

"To the one who has, more will be given, and he will have an abundance, but from the one who has not, even what he has will be taken away."

—MATTHEW 13:12

"For it is just like a man about to go on a journey, who called his own slaves and entrusted his possessions to them. To one he gave five talents, to another, two, to another, one, each according to his own ability; and he went on his journey. Immediately the one who had received the five talents went and traded with them, and gained five more talents. In the same manner the one who had received the two talents gained two more. But he who received the one talent went away, and dug a hole in the ground and hid his master's money.

"Now after a long time the master of those slaves came and settled accounts with them. The one who had received the five talents came up and brought five more talents, saying, 'Master, you entrusted five talents to me. See, I have gained five more talents.' His master said to him, 'Well done, good and faithful slave. You were faithful with a few things, I will put you in charge of many things; enter into the joy of your master.'

"Also the one who had received the two talents came up and said, 'Master, you entrusted two talents to me. See, I have gained two more talents.' His master said to him, 'Well done, good and faithful slave. You were faithful with a few things, I will put you in charge of many things; enter into the joy of your master.'

"And the one also who had received the one talent came up and said, 'Master, I knew you to be a hard man, reaping where you did not sow and gathering where you scattered no seed. And I was afraid, and went away and hid your talent in the ground. See, you have what is yours.'

"But his master answered and said to him, 'You wicked, lazy slave, you knew that I reap where I did not sow and gather where I scattered no seed. Then you ought to have put my money in the bank, and on my arrival I would have received my money back with interest. Therefore take away the talent from him, and give it to the one who has the ten talents.'

"For to everyone who has, more shall be given, and he will have an abundance; but from the one who does not have, even what he does have shall be taken away. Throw out the worthless slave into the outer darkness; in that place there will be weeping and gnashing of teeth.'" (Matt. 25:14–30 NASB95)

The parables of Jesus remind us of the universal truth that economics shows up wherever there are human beings in society. Certain economic patterns appear regularly, if not constantly, in human activity. The Bible confronts issues of saving versus spending, profit and gain, investment and loss, real estate and commerce and agriculture.

The parable of the talents in Matthew 25 is often misunderstood as being primarily about finance and stewardship. It is not, though the background of investing sets the structure of the parable. This is a parable about the kingdom and the work we are assigned within it. It's about how the kingdom works, and what the king expects of his subjects or, put another way, what the king has every right to expect of us.

Jesus began the parable by saying that his return will be like a man returning from a journey. Before his departure, the man had called his slaves and given them each an assignment to take care of during his absence. This man wisely wanted to see his assets at work, bringing him an increase during his travels. So, he entrusted his property to his slaves, but not evenly. He knew the abilities and giftedness of these slaves, and it was on the basis of his evaluation that he distributed his property to be invested. To one of the slaves, he gave five talents, to another he gave two, and to the third he gave only one, "each according to his own ability."

The man then went away, and the slaves bore the responsibility for their stewardship. There is no indication exactly how long the master would be gone, but it would be long enough that he would expect some financial gain upon his return. The slave who had received five talents put them to work in the investment marketplace, doubling the investment. A 100 percent return on an investment is spectacular. The first slave did extremely well, more than living up to the man's high expectations in entrusting to him the larger share of his possessions before he left.

The second slave was given only two talents, but he also doubled the investment, making two talents more. We're not told exactly how he did so, but there's no insinuation that there was anything other than proper investment and stewardship, which again resulted in a significant gain. The first two slaves had together received seven talents, doubling their portion of the master's investment to fourteen talents.

But everything changes when we turn to the third slave who had received just one talent. This slave merely dug a hole in the ground and hid the master's money. Clearly, there would be no gain. This is the equivalent of the Depression-era practice of putting money in the mattress. Generally speaking, it does nothing but lose value.

Predictably, the man returned from the journey and expected an accounting. Jesus shared that the slave who had received the five talents came forward eagerly reporting, "Master, you entrusted five talents to me. See, I have gained five more talents." The master's response is actually one of the greatest blessings found anywhere in the four Gospels. In the voice of the master in this parable, Jesus said, "Well done, good and faithful slave. You were faithful with a few things, I will put you in charge of many things; enter into the joy of your master."

What statement of affirmation and confirmation could exceed this master's invitation to "Enter into the joy of your master"? The master was supremely pleased with this slave. He affirmed the slave's stewardship by telling him that he had done well, and declaring him to be both "good and faithful." Consider the other parables of Jesus in which the slaves were anything but good and faithful. Consider the reality that we know this parable is a picture of the kingdom, and here we are told exactly what faithfulness looks like: serving the master in such a way that we increase his joy and are then invited to share it.

As the parable continues, the slave who had been given the two talents also came forward. He was glad to report, "Master, you entrusted two talents to me. See, I have gained two more talents." As he did the first, the master described the second slave as good and faithful and congratulated him on having been found faithful with a few things. The master then promised that he would be "put in charge of many things." Like the first slave, he received the ultimate confirmation from the master: "Enter into the joy of your master." At this point we understand the pattern, and we can anticipate that the master's response to the third slave is going to be quite different. We know already that he merely hid the talent in a hole in the ground, but we do not yet know the rationale. This third slave came forward to give his report, saying, "Master, I knew you to be a hard man, reaping where you did not sow and gathering where you scattered no seed. And I was afraid, and went away and hid your talent in the ground. See, you have what is yours."

Before proceeding further, we need to understand the inherent contradiction in what this man was reporting. He stated right up front that he knew his master to have exact and high expectations. He knew already that he had been expected to increase the investment, but he did no such thing. Instead, he blamed his action on the master himself, describing him to be "a hard man, reaping where you did not sow and gathering where you scattered no seed." In other words, he seemed to be saying that he believed himself to have no ability to meet the master's rightful expectation, so he simply put the investment in the ground, where, if it would experience no gain, it would at least not be lost.

It is a pathetic picture of irresponsibility and unfaithfulness.

The master responded with words of absolute condemnation: "You wicked, lazy slave, you knew that I reap where I did not sow and gather where I scattered no seed. Then you ought to have put my money in the bank, and on my arrival I would have received my money back with interest." It turns out that Jewish society in the first century was acquainted with banks and interests. Furthermore, this man condemned the slave who had stewardship over one talent because he could and should have invested it in a bank, even if he was anxious about his ability to handle the markets. The master's rebuke was biting, and it was final. This man was not to be given another chance. Instead, the master instructed his slaves to take the talent away from this man and instead give it to the first slave who had started with five talents and had increased the investment to ten. Jesus then concluded, "For to everyone who has, more shall be given, and he will have an abundance; but from the one who does not have, even what he does have shall be taken away."

That is the same lesson Jesus had shared with the disciples when they asked him why he spoke in parables, as we have seen in our consideration of Matthew 13. But the last words of Jesus' parable are words of the most horrifying judgment: "Throw out the worthless slave into the outer darkness; in that place there will be weeping and gnashing of teeth."

These words of final and irreversible judgment are well known to us by now. From the beginning of Jesus' teaching through parables, this warning has been constantly in the background. Judgment is coming and all humanity will be divided between those who belong to Christ and those who are sent to a place of eternal judgment where there will be weeping and gnashing of teeth—a graphic picture of absolute agony and excruciating torment.

When English translations refer to the unit of investment as a talent, our ears immediately jump to *talent* as in a human ability. Countless messages have been preached encouraging Christians in the English-speaking world to be good stewards of the talents and abilities that God has given us. That mandate is most assuredly true, and we are going to be judged concerning our stewardship of our talents and abilities to the glory of God. But, in this case the word *talent* is merely a transliteration of the original Greek *talanton*, which usually refers to a unit of measure, but can correspond to a unit of currency.

So, Jesus was actually talking about money. But what was his point? Surely, Jesus was not advising his followers concerning market investments. No, that is not the point of the parable.

We know that this parable is about the kingdom of heaven, and it is told in the context of Jesus' warning that his coming will be unexpected and sudden when it happens. Like the servants who were held to account as soon as this man returned from his journey, so Jesus will demand a report from his church.

Read rightly, this parable must be about our proper stewardship of opportunities for the kingdom. Though our human ability or giftedness is not the point of the parable, our human opportunity to make an increase in God's kingdom is very much the issue at stake. Every one of us has been given an opportunity to help build the kingdom of heaven in the service of our Lord Jesus Christ. Every single one of us has been invested with opportunity, even as the Lord judges our ability to fulfill that calling.

The issue of calling is vitally important. In the Reformation of the sixteenth century, Martin Luther and the other reformers stressed the notion of vocation, affirming that every single Christian is given a divine calling in Christ's service. This doctrine of vocation was a corrective to the Roman Catholic notion of a called priesthood over an uncalled laity. Luther came to the biblical conclusion that it was not just those serving the church directly who had been called by God, but that every single Christian received a calling within the larger context of God's purposes in his kingdom. As Luther stated, the milkmaid had a calling just as much as the preacher.

Economists and historians argued that the Protestant notion of vocation transformed the economy of the Western world. Max Weber and others referred to this Protestant theological principle as the Protestant work ethic. The world of work was transformed by the concept of calling, with Christians coming to understand that our responsibility is to answer that call in such a way that brings the kingdom greatest increase and brings our Master greatest glory.

The fact that there will be an accounting expected of us is important news. When Jesus returns, he expects to find his church faithful and at work in the cause of the kingdom. He has left us with incalculable opportunities for the advance of the kingdom. He has given us assignments including his charge to make disciples of all the nations. Every time we plant a church, every time we share the gospel with an unbeliever, every time we start a Bible study, every time we provide an opportunity for Christians to grow in grace and for unbelievers to hear the gospel, we are fulfilling our stewardship on behalf of the kingdom.

As a boy, I heard the examples of Christians such as George Muller (1805–1898) who started the Ashley Down orphanage in Bristol, England, and served as such a model of Christian compassion and devotional faithfulness. I remember hearing about Hudson Taylor (1832–1905), who started what was known as the China Inland Mission. His commitment to the expansion of Christ's kingdom was reflected in a letter he wrote on February 14, 1860, to his sister, Amelia Hudson Taylor. In that letter he stated, "If I had a thousand pounds, China should have it—if I had a thousand lives, China should have them. No! Not China, but Christ. Can we do too much for him? Can we do enough for such a precious savior?"[1]

I think of the example of John Wesley (1703–1791), the founder of World Methodism, who declared boldly, "The world is my parish." In a journal entry written on June 11, 1739, Wesley reflected: "I look upon all the world as my parish; thus far I mean, that in whatsoever part of it I am, I judge it meet, right, and my bounden duty to declare unto all that are willing to hear, the glad tidings of salvation."[2]

Throughout the history of the Christian church, we see such examples, beginning in the New Testament itself. Consider the book of Acts and the apostolic age. Trace the growth of the early church in those first decades after the death, burial, resurrection, and ascension of the Lord Jesus Christ. Consider the spectacular growth of Christianity in much of the world. Think about the fact that by most estimates there are more Christians living in China today than there are members of the Chinese communist party. Think about your own local area as well—of churches planted, of sermons preached, of testimonies given, and of efforts and opportunities for the kingdom that have been faithfully fulfilled.

We hear the severe words of divine judgment in this parable. What could be worse than to hear when Jesus returns, "Take the talent from him"?

Notice also that Jesus repeated the principle of the kingdom that he stated earlier in Matthew 13: "For to the one who has, more will be given, and he will have an abundance, but from the one who has not, even what he has will be taken away" (v. 12). We saw that law first applied to the hearing of the gospel itself. Now we see the same principle applied to our stewardship of kingdom responsibility. In both cases, the message is abundantly clear. The one who is faithful will receive more, while the faithless will lose everything.

Our great aspiration as Christians should be to hear the affirmation that comes from this master to his faithful slaves: "Well done, good and faithful slave. You were faithful with a few things, I will put you in charge of many things; enter into the joy of your master." Isn't that what we all really want? Isn't that what every one of us yearns for? To enter into the joy of our master? It will be by grace. It will be to God's glory, and it will be joy inexpressible.

# 14

## So Also My Heavenly Father Will Do to You

### THE PARABLE OF THE UNFORGIVING SERVANT

Be kind to one another, tenderhearted, forgiving one another, as God in Christ forgave you.

—EPHESIANS 4:32

"Everyone to whom much was given, of him much will be required."

—LUKE 12:48

Then Peter came up and said to him, "Lord, how often will my brother sin against me, and I forgive him? As many as seven times?" Jesus said to him, "I do not say to you seven times, but seventy-seven times.

"Therefore the kingdom of heaven may be compared to a king who wished to settle accounts with his servants. When he began to settle, one was brought to him who owed him ten thousand talents. And since he could not pay, his master ordered him to be sold, with his wife and children and all that he had, and payment to be made. So the servant fell on his knees, imploring him, 'Have patience with me, and I will pay you everything.' And out of pity for him, the master of that servant released him and forgave him the debt. But when that same servant went out, he found one of his fellow servants who owed him a hundred denarii, and seizing him, he began to choke him, saying, 'Pay what you owe.' So his fellow servant fell down and pleaded with him, 'Have patience with me, and I will pay you.' He refused and went and put him in prison until he should pay the debt. When his fellow servants saw what had taken place, they were greatly distressed, and they went and reported to their master all that had taken place. Then his master summoned him and said to him, 'You wicked servant! I forgave you all that debt because you pleaded with me. And should not you have had mercy on your fellow servant, as I had mercy on you?' And in anger his master delivered him to the jailers, until he should pay all his debt. So also my heavenly Father will do to every one of you, if you do not forgive your brother from your heart." (Matt. 18:21–35)

Matthew 16 is often identified as the "great constitution" of the church. In this famous passage, Jesus declared his church, and promised, "On this rock I will build my church and the gates of hell shall not prevail against it" (v. 18). There is a sense in which the church existed as soon as Christ began his public ministry and began calling disciples to himself. But the church age was declared openly only when Jesus asked the disciples, "But who do you say that I am?" You recall that it was Simon, soon to be renamed Peter, who responded, "You are the Christ, the Son of the living God" (vv. 15–16). It was upon that confession that Christ declared the establishment of his church. And it was by his own sovereign power that he declared that the gates of hell shall never prevail against it.

Immediately after declaring the existence of the church and offering the promise of its eternal preservation, Jesus told the disciples, "I will give you the keys of the kingdom of heaven, and whatever you bind on earth shall be bound in heaven, and whatever you loose on earth shall be loosed in heaven" (v. 19). Here we see the vital power of the "keys." Jesus gave the church the keys of the kingdom, as well as the power of binding and loosing. Those words are no longer commonplace today, but they were central to the experience of Israel. Israel was bound by the law and it was freed (or loosed) by the law. To be bound by the law was to be restricted, but to be loosed by the law was to be liberated. In other words, like ancient Israel, the church is bound to the Word of God, and we are bound by the Word of God, but the Word "looses" us to obedience. Binding and loosing in this sense describes what we now know as church discipline, the maintenance of church order and the vital issue of the accountability of disciples. As the Belgic Confession acknowledges, without discipline as a necessary mark of the church, there is no church.

Just two chapters later, Jesus would speak to his disciples about life and fellowship within the church, among brothers and sisters in Christ. In Matthew 18:15–20, Jesus gave instructions for what we are to do when a brother sins against us:

> If your brother sins against you, go and tell him his fault, between you and him alone. If he listens to you, you have gained your brother.

But if he does not listen, take one or two others along with you, that every charge may be established by the evidence of two or three witnesses. If he refuses to listen to them, tell it to the church. And if he refuses to listen even to the church, let him be to you as a Gentile and a tax collector. Truly, I say to you, whatever you bind on earth shall be bound in heaven, and whatever you loose on earth shall be loosed in heaven. Again, I say to you, if two of you agree on earth about anything they ask, it will be done for them by my father in heaven. For where two or three are gathered in my name, there am I among them.

Jesus told his disciples that when a brother commits sin against them, they are first to seek to make peace with this brother (or sister) in private. This is something that should be routine among Christians if we experience sin, either as the sinner or as the one who has been sinned against. We are to seek to handle the matter privately in order to preserve the relationship. On the basis of Scripture and mutual accountability before Christ, brothers and sisters should be able to work these things out. But the key issue here is not mere etiquette; it is forgiveness.

Forgiveness is one of the strongest words in the Bible. When we are told that God forgives sins, we do not read that he merely discounts sin and its consequences. It says that he utterly forgives. His forgiveness is absolute. Indeed, the Bible tells us that when we experience forgiveness, God does not even remember our sin. In the words of the psalmist, "As far as the east is from the west, so far does he remove our transgressions from us" (Ps. 103:12). That is an absolutely glorious promise. Forgiveness means the cancellation of the debt. It means the nullification of the wrongdoing. It means the restoration of the relationship and the recovery of fellowship. This is true between the sinner and God, made possible through the atoning sacrifice of the Lord Jesus Christ. But this forgiveness is also to take place among Christian brothers and sisters.

It's a simple fact that sin will happen, even among Christians. Given that our sanctification is yet incomplete and our sin nature is all too real, we still sin, sometimes against our brothers and sisters in Christ. Jesus' instruction to us when we are sinned against is that we are to forgive. But if there is no confession and forgiveness asked for, even when you "take one or two others along with you," then the matter is to be taken to the church. Remember that Jesus' instructions concerning sin and forgiveness between brothers and sisters in Christ came just two chapters after he had declared his church, and now we are being told already about how life inside the church is to be lived faithfully. As Jesus made clear in this passage, the stakes in the matter of forgiveness (or a lack of forgiveness) are massive.

Matthew's gospel then immediately takes us into a passage in which Peter, the disciple who had confessed that Jesus is the Christ, the Son of the living God, approached Jesus after this teaching on the forgiveness of a brother and asked, "Lord, how often will my brother sin against me, and I forgive him? As many as seven times?" Jesus responded to him, "I do not say to you seven times, but seventy-seven times."

Peter's question was not merely hypothetical, as if he were asking something that might be offered in a law school discussion. This was a question asked inside the church, among the disciples, about sin and forgiveness among brothers and sisters in Christ. It is easy to look at Peter's question and see it as foolish, insolent, and ridiculous. But in its context this is a legitimate question. What is the demand of forgiveness now? To what extent must we extend this forgiveness?

When Peter suggested seven times, he was offering what he believed to be an exaggerated number. In Scripture, seven has a high symbolic significance, often indicating completeness and perfection. Indeed, Peter's suggestion of forgiving up to seven times is grounded in biblical numerology. We are told that God made the heavens and the earth in six days, and then rested on the seventh from all the work he had done (Gen. 2:3). In Genesis 4:24, we are told of Lamech killing another man in self-defense. Later, he told his wives, "If Cain's revenge is sevenfold, then Lamech's is seventy-sevenfold." Lamech justified himself by referring back to Cain and Abel in Genesis 4:15. He made a plea before God based upon God's grace extended to Cain. If Cain was to be avenged sevenfold, even though he murdered his own brother, then surely God should be merciful to him for murdering another man out of self-defense. This pattern of sevenfold versus seventy-sevenfold was thus already part of the Jewish imagination. Peter was aware of it, as was Jesus.

This is the context for Jesus taking Peter's outer estimate and expanding it exponentially beyond our moral imagination. Clearly, Jesus was telling Peter that we are always to forgive a brother. There is no statute of limitations. There is no limit to the forgiveness that is expected of us. We are to extend grace and forgiveness without limit, precisely because God's grace and mercy has been extended to us without limit, and thus we are saved.

Jesus' words to Peter were meant to help him (and all of us) understand grace. True forgiveness does not keep count. God's grace and mercy are infinite. Peter seemed to want a number in order to calibrate his conscience. Jesus responded by telling Peter that he would receive no number. However, Peter would receive a parable.

The parable of the unforgiving servant comes in the context of this conversation between Jesus and his disciples about the forgiveness of a brother. That context is crucial, framing our habits of forgiveness toward one another within the reality that we are the recipients of God's infinite forgiveness.

Jesus began this parable like so many others: with a kingdom of God comparison statement. In this parable, the kingdom of God is like a king who wanted to settle accounts with his servants. The disciples would have well understood this legal situation. Kings periodically chose to settle accounts just to clear the table and set things right. The kind of king the disciples would have imagined in this story would have been one of the many vassal kings who served not as monarchs over great empires but as local monarchs over a community or territory. In such a context, the king would often have personal knowledge of his subjects.

When this king decided that he was going to settle accounts, one particular man was brought before him who owed him ten thousand talents. That was an extraordinary debt. It represented a debt that no normal citizen could ever hope to repay. For this man, the situation was hopeless. And since he could not pay, he was to be forced into servanthood and the proceeds used to pay off at least a portion of his debt.

Knowing what was at stake, the man dropped to his knees and pleaded with the king that he, along with his wife and children, be spared. He implored him, saying: "Have patience with me, and I will pay you everything." The king felt pity toward the man and released him and forgave him the massive debt. Here we have a picture of grace and forgiveness.

We should ponder the significance of how so much of our understanding of the atonement comes down to the payment of a debt. Indebtedness may refer to borrowed money, but it can also indicate a violation of honor. We transgress against God's law and we dishonor him by our disobedience. We create debts that we could never hope to pay. All of that is in the background of the doctrine of atonement as set out in the New Testament. The debt will have to be paid, and Christ paid the due penalty for our sin by shedding his blood on the cross. The Bible speaks of our debts being wiped away, and we are told to pray for forgiveness by asking for our debts to be forgiven, even as we forgive our debtors. When it comes to forgiveness, the language of debt is always in the foreground.

In other words, just a few lines into the parable, we already know that this king symbolizes God, and the forgiveness extended by the king, beyond all moral claim, points directly to the forgiveness that sinners are given by God through Christ.

The parable then shifts and the central character becomes the man who had been forgiven his insurmountable debt. He, along with his wife and children, had been rescued from a horrifying predicament, and a debt he could never hope to repay had been effectively wiped clean by the king. But upon his release, the same servant went out and found a fellow servant who owed him one hundred denarii, a tiny fraction of the debt he had owed the king. He grabbed his fellow servant, seizing him and choking him, and demanded, "Pay what you owe." This man had just been on his knees pleading his case before a merciful king, and now his fellow servant was doing the same with him, begging, "Have patience with me, and I will pay you."

The promise this fellow servant made to repay the debt was not unreasonable. A working man could have eventually paid off a debt of one hundred denarii, something like one hundred days of wages. He promised his fellow servant that he would repay the debt if the fellow servant would merely extend him patience. Notice that this man did not even really demand mercy, just patience. Nevertheless, the servant who had just been forgiven much refused and then placed the other servant in prison until he could pay the debt.

Throughout most of human history, prisons have not been places where criminals were held in confinement, but rather where debtors were held until they could repay their debt. That is precisely the context we see here when this servant is forced into prison by his fellow servant.

The next turn in the parable takes place when the other servants observed what had just taken place and became "greatly distressed." We can understand their distress. They had just seen the first man be forgiven a debt he could never hope to repay, experiencing mercy that freed him from a sentence he could never have overcome. But having just received extravagant mercy and grace, this servant refused to extend even a fraction of that grace to his fellow servant. The other servants were infuriated and outraged. They reported to the king, their master, "all that had taken place."

At this point judgment falls conclusively. The master summoned the man back and said, "I forgave you all that debt because you pleaded with me. And should you not have had mercy on your fellow servant, as I had mercy on you?" Then, in anger, the master delivered the servant to the jailers until he should pay off all his debt.

This is a comparison parable. Jesus put before us two different debts on the part of two different individuals. The king responded with mercy and forgiveness. The man just forgiven, by comparison, responded with an absolute refusal to demonstrate grace. Forgiveness is at the forefront here. The master offered forgiveness, but the servant offered none. They become contrasting pictures of grace and graceless-ness, and Jesus brought down the hammer of divine judgment with a force that is shocking and bracing even now. The man who had experienced forgiveness but then refused to forgive had his own forgiveness canceled. He was thrown into prison until he could repay the debt—a debt we all know he could never repay.

The finality of this judgment was made even clearer when Jesus turned to the disciples and said, "So also my heavenly Father will do to every one of you, if you do not forgive your brother from your heart."

Jesus' statement raises the stakes. Not only must we forgive our brother and sister, but we must forgive them "from [our] heart." The Gospel of John tells us that Jesus could read human hearts (John 2:24–25). God knows our hearts; he knows when we have forgiven and when we merely pretend to have forgiven.

If God has merely pretended to forgive us, then we are doomed. But we have confidence that the forgiveness God has extended to us is absolute, the conditions of that forgiveness have been completely accomplished in the atonement of the Lord Jesus Christ. When God forgives our sin, he indeed separates our sin from us as far as the east is from the west. And this comes from the saving heart of God.

Christians are told that the demand on us is not mere forgiveness, as if it could be offered through clenched teeth. No, we must offer true forgiveness from our hearts, precisely because we know, and can never for a moment forget, the grace and forgiveness we have received from God—infinite mercy.

We cannot leave this parable without pondering what it means that the forgiveness demanded here is the forgiveness of a brother. The context is clearly the church, so much so that Jesus said that if a private conversation does not bring about restoration, and neither does bringing two or three godly, wise witnesses into the matter, we are to take the issue to the church. We see similar language later in the Gospel of Matthew, and we are constantly reminded that this kingdom ethic is addressed to the sons and daughters of the kingdom. This does not mean we do not have a responsibility to forgive non-Christians who sin against us. But it does emphasize that sons and daughters of the kingdom, the children of light, have a special responsibility to forgive one another, precisely because of our shared experience of infinite forgiveness in Christ.

Jesus offers in this parable a picture of the kingdom, which brings both threat and promise to believers. The demonstration of God's grace is abundant and obvious, but the reality of God's judgment is also clear.

Consider the verdict coming from the master in two different parables. In the parable of the talents, the master described the two servants who had fulfilled their responsibility as good and faithful and invited them to "enter into the joy of your master." Compare that with Jesus' words that conclude the parable of the unforgiving servant: "So also my heavenly Father will do to every one of you, if you do not forgive your brother, from your heart."

Let's be honest: we want to enter into the joy of our Master. But this means that we who have received infinite forgiveness in Christ must offer limitless forgiveness to our brothers and sisters in Christ.

# 15

# The Kingdom of Heaven Is Like This

## PARABLES OF KINGDOM REALITY, CRISIS, AND POWER

So Pilate entered his headquarters again and called Jesus and said to him, "Are you the King of the Jews?" . . . Jesus answered, "My kingdom is not of this world. If my kingdom were of this world, my servants would have been fighting, that I might not be delivered over to the Jews. But my kingdom is not from the world." Then Pilate said to him, "So you are a king?" Jesus answered, "You say that I am a king."

—JOHN 18:33–37

From that time Jesus began to preach, saying, "Repent, for the kingdom of heaven is at hand."

—MATTHEW 4:17

"With what can we compare the kingdom of God, or what parable shall we use for it?" (Mark 4:30)

He put another parable before them, saying, "The kingdom of heaven is like a grain of mustard seed that a man took and sowed in his field. It is the smallest of all seeds, but when it has grown it is larger than all the garden plants and becomes a tree, so that the birds of the air come and make nests in its branches." (Matt. 13:31–32)

He told them another parable. "The kingdom of heaven is like leaven that a woman took and hid in three measures of flour, till it was all leavened." (Matt. 13:33)

"The kingdom of heaven is like treasure hidden in a field, which a man found and covered up. Then in his joy he goes and sells all that he has and buys that field." (Matt. 13:44)

"Again, the kingdom of heaven is like a merchant in search of fine pearls, who, on finding one pearl of great value, went and sold all that he had and bought it." (Matt. 13:45–46)

"Again, the kingdom of heaven is like a net that was thrown into the sea and gathered fish of every kind. When it was full, men drew it ashore and sat down and sorted the good into containers but threw away the bad. So it will be at the end of the age. The angels will come out and separate the evil from the righteous and throw them into the fiery furnace. In that place there will be weeping and gnashing of teeth." (Matt. 13:47–50)

"Have you understood all these things?" They said to him,

"Yes." And he said to them, "Therefore every scribe who has been trained for the kingdom of heaven is like a master of a house, who brings out of his treasure what is new and what is old." (Matt. 13:51–52)

As we have seen, each of the parables of Jesus is a parable of grace, a parable of judgment, and a parable of the kingdom. Each parable displays a reality of the kingdom, offers a glimpse of the very nature of the kingdom of heaven, and reveals how to enter it. Of course, we also understand that it is none other than the King who is describing his own kingdom.

In the Gospel of Matthew, we encounter a series of short, graphic parables by which Jesus described his kingdom. Each offers a potent lesson for us, and taken together they offer us stunning insights into Christ's kingdom, the kingdom of heaven, and how we are to see it and long for it in this life. Beyond this, these parables of the kingdom tell us a great deal about how Christians are to live in this world until Christ comes.

## The Parable of the Mustard Seed

In Matthew 13:31–32, Jesus shared the parable of the mustard seed. The mustard seed is a very small seed indeed, and this parable is a short parable. Jesus told them, "The kingdom of heaven is like a grain of mustard seed that a man took and sowed in his field. It is the smallest of all seeds, but when it has grown it is larger than all the garden plants and becomes a tree, so that the birds of the air come and make their nests in its branches."

Once again, a metaphor from agriculture serves to show us a king-dom reality. In this case it is a very potent seed. In the same chapter, Jesus had told his disciples the parable of the sower in which the key issue had been the soils. Of course, the soils only became important because of the potency of the seed. Now, in this very short parable, Jesus was looking at the seed itself. The kingdom of heaven is like the smallest seed that grows explosively to become one of the biggest plants.

Jesus didn't explain a great deal about what happens between when the man sows the seed and the fully grown plant appears. That narra-tion was unnecessary. It is the picture itself that looms before us as the great issue. Never underestimate the kingdom. Never believe that when you look at what appears to be a very small spiritual reality it will stay small. Never believe that what we might consider to be the smallest act of faithfulness is going to be understood in the kingdom as a small act. Just like the widow's mite turned out to be huge, it turns out that the kingdom grows explosively from small things.

It also turns out that the kingdom has to be evaluated in kingdom terms. A failure to understand this has often led to fatal miscalculation. It is said that Joseph Stalin, the murderous "Man of Steel" and Soviet leader, having been told of the pope's opposition to his expansion of Soviet influence into the East, snorted with a dismissive response: "How many divisions has the pope?" The point here is not the pope but Stalin's absolute dismissal of any spiritual power as being a threat to his massive armies, by then victorious with the Allies over Nazi Germany. We get his point and we can see his sneer.

How many divisions has the church? Where is our army? Where are our tanks and missiles? Where is the power of the kingdom dis-played? A text like this warns us not to look for spiritual realities to show up in earthly statistics and in what the world sees as powerful and important.

Just as it is all too easy to dismiss the mustard seed because it appears so small, the reality is that it will grow into a massive plant, so large that it is described as a tree. That tree is described as a part of God's "peaceable kingdom" in which the birds of the air come and make their nests in its branches.

The kingdom of God is just like the mustard seed. In earthly terms, it appears quite small, but in eternal terms it is already present and will soon arrive in fullness.

# The Parable of the Leaven

Jesus moved from speaking of the mustard seed to speaking of leaven— another short parable. Jesus identified both an elaborate parable (such as the parable of the sower) and a one-sentence parable (such as the parable of the leaven) as being genuine parables. Each is a picture. Just like we should not underestimate the mustard seed, we had better not underestimate a short parable of Jesus. "The kingdom of heaven is like leaven that a woman took and hid in three measures of flour, till it was all leavened." The making of bread was once a central fact of life for virtually all families. Only in more recent times has bread become something most of us buy in a store or in a bakery. Furthermore, in the age before preservatives, bread had to be made daily, otherwise it was of no use. In both the Old and New Testaments, the metaphor of bread is inescapable and often takes center stage. In John 6, Jesus described his own identity as bread when he declared, "I am the bread of life." Jesus stated: "'Truly, truly, I say to you, it was not Moses who gave you the bread from heaven, but my Father gives you the true bread from heaven. For the bread of God is he who comes down from heaven and gives life to the world.' They said to him, 'Sir, give us this bread always.'

Jesus said to them, 'I am the bread of life; whoever comes to me shall not hunger, and whoever believes in me shall never thirst'" (vv. 32–35).

So, just as Israel survived in the wilderness as they were fed manna, the bread of God, so we as Christians come to saving faith in the Lord Jesus Christ as we receive the Bread of Life, and thus depend on him entirely for our salvation.

The bread described in this parable is bread that has risen, and that means the yeast has done its work. For the daily making of bread, a portion of the leaven used in making the loaves would be retained so that it could be used the next day in order to produce more rising bread. The yeast does its work in a way that creates the leavening effect. The yeast is contagious and infectious, in effect, spreading throughout the entire mass of grain such that under the right circumstances, the explosive power of the leaven produces a risen loaf ready for baking.

In the parable Jesus told, the leaven is a lump that is hidden in three measures of flour, and in due time, all the flour was leavened. Anyone who knows this process understands that we do not get to directly see the yeast at work in the leavening process and we do not get to see the leaven in the explosion of its work. What we do see is the result. What had been a small lump becomes a large loaf. The yeast does its work invisibly, but it produces an undeniably visible result.

Jesus said that the kingdom of heaven is just like this. It looks small but grows to immense size. Again, the growth happens by an explosive power that is outside the control of the farmer or of the bread-maker. The power is in the seed or in the leaven. Neither the seed nor the leaven looks particularly powerful. And yet, we have food to eat precisely because this explosive growth happens.

Put together, these two parables serve to underline the fact that even Christians often underestimate and misunderstand the kingdom of Christ. We want to see visible evidence. Like the disciples, we want to see the kingdom established and we want Christ to reign in such a way that, right now *every* knee will bow and every tongue will confess that Jesus Christ is Lord. We want to see righteousness and justice established in full measure *right now.* We want to see God's kingdom come and his will be done, *now.*

But the Father has his reasons for the delay of Christ's coming. Jesus was telling his disciples not to mistake this delay for a denial of the kingdom. God's will is not being frustrated, and all things are unfolding according to his perfect plan. He alone knows the timing, and in his good, sovereign time all things will be accomplished, including the return of the Lord Jesus Christ and the establishment of his kingdom in its fullness.

Until then, and this is vitally important, we do get to see the kingdom as it is already here. We do see the promise of the kingdom, but it appears in ways that the world would never understand. We see the advance of the kingdom when a single sinner comes to faith in the Lord Jesus Christ. Just as Jesus told us in Luke 15, when even one sinner repents there is great joy in heaven. That repentance reflects a spiritual power that is greater than anything any human empire or government could ever muster. One single conversion is a more powerful reality than the splitting of the atom. It is hard sometimes for Christians to keep this in mind, but Jesus told the disciples these parables in order that they would not be frustrated by the fact that the kingdom comes on God's own terms and in his own time.

## The Parable of the Hidden Treasure

Just a few verses later, Jesus told the disciples: "The kingdom of heaven is like treasure hidden in a field, which a man found and covered up.

Then in his joy he goes and sells all that he has and buys that field."
This might sound like an unlikely business transaction, but it makes
perfect sense if you follow the logic of the parable. A man hid a treasure
in the field, and only he knew it was there. His plan was to buy the field,
so that he would gain the treasure. If it was on the property he bought,
then it would be his.

Jesus offered no further details about the treasure or the field. We
know nothing further about the man. Neither the man nor the treasure
nor the field is important in any detail. Rather, the parable is about the
fact that a man knew he had something of such surpassing value that
he sold all he had in order to buy the field and gain the treasure.

As in the case of other parables with financial illustrations, Jesus
was not offering business advice. This is not a lesson in real estate.
Instead, it is a powerful lesson about the surpassing treasure of the
kingdom of heaven. Jesus said that if we truly understand the kingdom
of heaven, we will sell all that we have in order to gain it. Once again,
the financial transaction is not what is important. The issue is the
priority of the kingdom and its all-surpassing greatness.

Human nature teaches us that people will do incredible things in
order to get what they want. Prisons are filled with people who did ille-
gal things in failed attempts to get what they wanted. Psychotherapists'
offices are also filled with people who did not get what they wanted,
and are seeking therapy in order to cope with that fact. All around us
are people who think themselves happy as they're building their lives
on earthly priorities, but they are missing the all-surpassing value of
the kingdom of heaven.

The Bible tells us that where our heart is, there also is our treasure,
and that is an inviolable principle of the kingdom (Matt. 6:21). Where
our treasure is, there our heart is also. Our heart is revealed in *what*
we treasure and in how urgently we pursue it. The man in this parable

clearly understood the value of the treasure he had hidden in a field, and he was willing to give up everything else he owned in order to gain it.

Over and over again Jesus would speak about the sacrifices that must be made on behalf of the kingdom. At times Jesus told the disciples that they would have to exchange earthly security for eternal heavenly security. Most Christians will forgo earthly riches, in order to gain heavenly riches. Some will even have to give up family for the sake of the kingdom. This man was willing to give up everything he had in order to gain the treasure hidden in the field. Jesus pointed out that every Christian must have the same priority about the kingdom of heaven. If we truly see the kingdom, and understand its all-surpassing value, then we will desire it and be willing to give up everything else for the sake of gaining it.

## The Parable of the Pearl of Great Value

Here we are given another one-sentence parable. Jesus said: "Again, the kingdom of heaven is like a merchant in search of fine pearls, who, on finding one pearl of great value, went and sold all that he had and bought it."

Pearls are among the most valuable items detailed in Scripture. As we know, the best pearls take many years to be produced and are found only within the shellfish who create the pearl, not by design but merely by biological operation. Like jewels, pearls are beautiful and scarce. It is that beauty matched with scarcity that creates the value.

In this parable, we meet a man who was a merchant in the business of fine pearls. Like an expert diamond-cutter recognizes a priceless diamond, this merchant recognized a priceless pearl. As he was searching through merchandise, he found one pearl of surpassing value. It was so valuable that he "went and sold all that he had and bought it." We don't have to be told that this is a direct parallel with the parable of the hidden treasure. But perhaps this also tells us something about ourselves, for Jesus has laid out not just one parable of this structure, but two. No doubt, we need both of these parables in order to get the point adequately.

The key issue here is of *desire*. Christians are often afraid of desire, precisely because we know how our earthly desires can be so ungodly and overpowering. Too many Christians speak of Christianity as a renunciation of desire. But this is profoundly untrue. Christianity is not about the denial of desire, but about the denial of the wrong desires in order to turn to a greater love, a greater desire, a greater obsession.

Plainly, we are to desire Christ. In Psalm 37:4, we are told, "Delight yourself in the LORD, and he will give you the desires of your heart." Notice that the psalmist did not say that we are to forgo delight and desire, but rather we are to calibrate them according to the kingdom of God.

This exchange of desire is made clear by the apostle Paul in his letter to the Philippians:

> But whatever gain I had, I counted as loss for the sake of Christ. Indeed, I count everything as loss because of the surpassing worth of knowing Christ Jesus my Lord. For his sake I have suffered the loss of all things and count them as rubbish, in order that I may gain Christ and be found in him, not having a righteousness of my own that comes from the law, but that which comes through faith in Christ, the righteousness from God that depends on faith—that I may know him and the power of his resurrection, and may share his sufferings, becoming like him in his death, that by any means possible I may attain the resurrection from the dead.
>
> (PHIL. 3:7–11)

These are some of the most precious words of testimony from the apostle Paul. But notice he spoke of the exchange of desire. He no longer desired the things that he was willing to count as loss for the sake of Christ. He had come to the point where he counted everything as loss because of "the surpassing worth of knowing Christ Jesus my Lord." He had exchanged one love for another, one desire for another.

As Augustine, the great theologian of the early church, and Jonathan Edwards, one of the greatest theological minds ever to serve the church, understood, we never actually turn to a lesser love. We only turn from a lesser love to a greater love.

Indeed, Augustine said:

> But living a just and holy life requires one to be capable of an objective and impartial evaluation of things: to love things, that is to say, in the right order, so that you do not love what is not to be loved, or fail to love what is to be loved, or have a greater love for what should be loved less, or an equal love for things that should be loved less or more, or to a lesser or greater love for things that should be loved equally.[1]

That language may sound complex, but Augustine was pointing to the Christian responsibility to order our loves according to Scripture. Our love of God must be the greatest of all loves, and then we will seek to love what God loves. We do not renounce all desire, as in Buddhism, but we are to discipline and calibrate our desires for the things above rather than the things below.

This recalibration, we should note, is seen in the great commandment of Christ in which we are told that the greatest commandment is to love the Lord our God with all our heart and soul and mind, and the second, like unto it, is to love our neighbor as ourselves

(Matt. 22:36–40). The right order of love is to love God first. Then, loving what God loves, we love our neighbor.

In these two parables, Jesus did not tell us to renounce desire, but to desire the kingdom of heaven like a treasure hidden in a field or a pearl of surpassing price. As I warned you, these two parables, each just a sentence long, are nothing less than explosive disclosures of God's kingdom.

## The Parable of the Net

Jesus gave us a different kind of parable when he described the kingdom of heaven as a net gathering fish. The parable is short, and it points to divine judgment. Jesus said:

> "Again, the kingdom of heaven is like a net that was thrown into the sea and gathered fish of every kind. When it was full, men drew it ashore and sat down and sorted the good into containers but threw away the bad. So it will be at the end of the age. The angels will come out and separate the evil from the righteous and throw them into the fiery furnace. In that place there will be weeping and gnashing of teeth."

Just as the pictures and stories drawn from agriculture would have been readily accessible to those who heard Jesus teach the parables, the same would be true of fishing stories. Fish have been one of the most important sources of protein for human beings throughout history. Fishing is not only a hobby; for human beings it has been nothing less than vital to life. There are different ways to go after fish, but commercial fishing requires using a net. The net described in this parable is a dragnet that is simply thrown into the water and then drawn together. Jesus spoke of evangelism in terms of his disciples being fishers of men.

Fishing nets and the gathering together of the fishes became a portrait of the kingdom.

But in this case the point of the parable is that the net drew in a catch that included both the worthy and the unworthy, the edible and the inedible. A sorting process was thus necessary, and we are told that the fishermen separated the good into containers but the bad were simply thrown away. Again, an easy story to understand, with a powerful picture that comes immediately to mind.

There is a judgment to come and there will be some who are received and some who are rejected. Jesus put it bluntly when he said that at the close of the age it is the angels who will come out and separate the evil from the righteous. The unrighteous will be thrown into the fiery furnace where there will be weeping and gnashing of teeth. We have seen this pattern of warning and the impending reality of divine judgment again and again. In the Gospel of Matthew, Jesus was abundantly clear that weeping and gnashing of teeth described the condition after judgment of those who are cast away into eternal punishment.

As in the parable of the weeds, there's a separation coming. In the parable of the net, the separation comes just as soon as the fish are gathered into the boat. Containers for the good fish, rejection for the bad fish. And the key, of course, to understanding this is that good and bad, righteous and unrighteous, point to those who are in Christ and those who are not. It is Christ's righteousness that will suffice. No human righteousness will do.

## Treasures Old and New

Jesus asked his disciples after teaching a sequence of parables, "Have you understood all these things?" In a sense, Jesus is asking his church this question all the time. The disciples told Jesus yes, they had understood the parables. I often think of conversations I had with my father when I was a boy. He would talk about something, often with a directive point, and then ask me, "Do you understand me?" I can never remember answering in the negative, because Dad had a way of making his point clear. He was a godly man, and I was his firstborn son. I loved spending time with him and listening to him talk. There were times when his conversations with me were extremely directive, and even corrective. But I knew that when he asked, "Did you understand me, son?" he was making a point even by asking the question. Dad did everything within his power to make sure that if there was a failure, it was not a failure of communication.

I raise those conversations with my father as I think about Jesus' question to his disciples, because I do remember, powerfully, that there were times when I would not truly understand what my father was telling me until some time after the conversation. There was a sense in which I *did* understand what he was telling me in the immediate context of the conversation. But there's another sense in which it took some time and reflection, perhaps even some experience, for me to understand, in a far deeper sense, what my father intended to communicate.

For the disciples, we know that there was a before and after to their understanding of what Jesus had taught them. Before his death, burial, and resurrection from the dead, the disciples surely understood what Jesus had been telling them, but only in part. On the other side of those saving events, Jesus' teachings became clearer and the disciples' understanding grew deeper.

In the parable of the treasures old and new, Jesus said to his disciples: "Therefore every scribe who has been trained for the kingdom of heaven is like a master of a house, who brings out of his treasure what is new and what is old." What was Jesus talking about here? In this short parable we encounter a dramatic display of the power of biblical theology. Jesus was speaking of the Old Testament scriptures, telling us that scribes trained for the kingdom of heaven will find in those scriptures things that are old, including the rightful interpretation of those Old Testament passages at the time, and things that are new, realizations of the fulfillment of prophecy and the promise of all the Scriptures in Christ.

We see in the pattern of promise and fulfillment that even the disciples understood the Old Testament Scriptures anew after the resurrection. This is displayed wonderfully in Luke 24, when we read about the two disciples walking on the road to Emmaus. On the way there, they were met by the resurrected Christ, whom they did not recognize. In the course of the conversation with the disciples, Jesus asked them, "Was it not necessary that the Christ should suffer these things and enter into his glory?" (v. 26). Then we are told that "beginning with Moses and all the Prophets, he interpreted to them in all the Scriptures the things concerning himself" (v. 27). So, Jesus taught his disciples the pattern of promise and fulfillment in the Scriptures. Jesus showed these disciples on the road to Emmaus the things old and the things new, drawn directly from the holy Scriptures.

Later, when the two men were alone, they said to each other, "Did not our hearts burn within us while he talked to us on the road, while he opened to us the Scriptures?" (v. 32). Those disciples recognized that their hearts had burned with joy in understanding, for the first time, the deeper meaning of those Old Testament promises as fulfilled in Christ. Every single text, every single verse, every single passage of the Old Testament points to Christ and is ultimately fulfilled in him. In the parable of the treasures new and old, Jesus was teaching his disciples to learn, as scribes train for the kingdom of heaven, what it means to read the Old Testament and to bring out treasure, "what is new and what is old."

# The Kingdom of Christ

All parables reveal the kingdom of heaven, which is the kingdom of Christ. When we talk about the kingdom of heaven and the kingdom of Christ and the kingdom of God, we're talking about God's reign, through the Son, throughout all eternity. God's kingdom means his rule, and we are not awaiting the inauguration of the kingdom of God. Our sovereign God is King, and he has never at any time been anything less than the King. Throughout eternity he reigns, and he will reign forevermore. His kingdom is wherever he is and wherever he is he rules.

When God sent his Son, incarnate in human flesh, he was sending the promised Messiah, who would rule from David's throne forever. Before Jesus began his earthly ministry, John declared, "The kingdom of heaven is at hand" (Matt. 3:2). He declared his own mission as preparing the way for the coming King. As Jesus began his earthly ministry, Mark tells us that "Jesus came into Galilee, proclaiming the gospel of God, and saying, 'The time is fulfilled, and the kingdom of God is at hand; repent and believe in the gospel'" (Mark 1:14–15).

Thus, the kingdom of God came into history in an entirely new dimension in the incarnation of the Lord Jesus Christ, who declared at the beginning of his ministry that the kingdom of God was indeed at hand. It was present because *he* was present. Throughout the Gospels, as Jesus taught his disciples and the gathering crowds about the kingdom of heaven, he spoke to them as the King. Throughout the Gospels, both the imagery and the substance of kingship would come up again and again in reference to Jesus. It was none other than the angel Gabriel who had declared these things to Mary, even as she was told that she would be the mother of the Christ. Gabriel had said unto her,

> "And behold, you will conceive in your womb and bear a son, and you shall call his name Jesus. He will be great and will be called the Son of the Most High. And the Lord God will give to him the throne of his father David, and he will reign over the house of Jacob forever, and of his kingdom there will be no end." (Luke 1:31–33)

The birth of Jesus in Bethlehem was the birth of a king, and his kingdom became more and more apparent in the course of his earthly ministry. His miracles and signs and teaching authority revealed him as King. This becomes crucial in the Gospel of John when Pilate asked Jesus straightforwardly, "Are you the King of the Jews?" In his exchange with Pilate, Jesus never denied being a king, but he did make clear that his kingdom is not of this world. Pilate failed to understand, asking him again, "So you are a king?" (18:33, 37). Yes, Pilate, Christ is not only King of kings, but Lord of lords.

At the conclusion of Matthew's gospel, we find the passage that is commonly known as the Great Commission, and in this passage, Jesus spoke of his royal sovereignty: "All authority in heaven and on earth has been given to me. Go therefore and make disciples of all nations, baptizing them in the name of the Father and of the Son and of the Holy Spirit, teaching them to observe all that I have commanded you. And behold, I am with you always, to the end of the age" (28:18–20). When Jesus claimed "all authority in heaven and on earth," he claimed kingship. In Philippians 2, Paul described the obedience of Christ, even unto death, and declared, "Therefore God has highly exalted him and bestowed on him the name that is above every name, so that at the name of Jesus every knee should bow, in heaven and on earth and under the earth, and every tongue confess that Jesus Christ is Lord, to the glory of God the Father" (vv. 9–11).

Rightly understood, the entire Bible points to God's rule of the cosmos through Christ. At the same time, the kingdom makes specific reference to those who, by redemption, have come to be united to Christ. In order to understand this distinction, we need to know that the kingship of Christ extends to both his *regnum potentiae* and his *regnum gratiae*, that is, his kingdom of dominion and his kingdom of grace.

The Bible makes clear that the kingship of Christ extends to the entire universe; this is his reign of dominion. Colossians 1 tells us that all things are under his dominion, all things created "in heaven and on earth, visible and invisible, whether thrones or dominions or rulers or authorities—all things are created through him and for him." Paul added, "And he is before all things, and in him all things hold together" (vv. 16–17). Christ, and Christ alone, holds all things together, even as he was the Word through whom all things were created. It is to Jesus that every knee will bow, and it is his name as Lord that every tongue will confess. Christ's rule of dominion demonstrates that there is not one atom or molecule or speck in the entire cosmos that is outside his kingly reign.

But Scripture puts greatest emphasis upon Christ's kingdom of grace, his rule of grace. This is clear even in the passage from Colossians, where after declaring that Christ is "before all things, and in him all things hold together," Paul added, "And he is the head of the body, the church. He is the beginning, the firstborn from the dead, that in everything he might be preeminent" (vv. 17–18). The kingdom of Christ is most importantly seen in his rule of grace by which sinners are redeemed and made right with God, sanctified, and eventually glorified.

The kingdom of grace is made visible in the church of the Lord Jesus Christ. Those who are citizens of the kingdom of grace come under the rule of Christ only by grace. As Louis Berkhof rightly observed, "No one is a citizen of this kingdom in virtue of his humanity. Only the redeemed have that honour and privilege. Christ paid the ransom for those that are His, and by His Spirit applies to them the merits of His perfect sacrifice. Consequently, they now belong to Him and recognize Him as their Lord and King."[2]

John Calvin was certainly correct when he said that it is the mission of the church to make the invisible kingdom visible in the world. And yet, at the same time, liberal theology deviated from the gospel when it sought to separate the kingdom of God from the message of redemption, exchanging the gospel of salvation for a message of social improvement, claimed to be the realization of the kingdom of God. The church, as Calvin taught, bears the responsibility to make the kingdom of Christ visible in this world by the assignment that is given to the church to preach and teach the gospel, to evangelize, to take the message of the gospel to the ends of the earth, to preach the Word of God in season and out of season, and to display in the church the marks of a redeemed people.

Such a church will make a real difference in the world for the cause of the gospel and for the glory of Christ. A faithful church will, by its existence in the gospel, make the kingdom of grace visible in a fallen world. The church is assigned a mission, and that mission includes good works even as we witness. But the church must never confuse the existing order for the kingdom of Christ, which has come as Christ has come, and is visible in the church even now, and one day will be fully realized as he comes in glory.

# 16

# When the Son of Man
# Comes in His Glory

## THE PARABLE OF THE SHEEP AND THE GOATS

Then I saw a great white throne and him who was seated on it. From his presence earth and sky fled away, and no place was found for them. And I saw the dead, great and small, standing before the throne, and the books were opened. Then another book was opened, which is the book of life. And the dead were judged by what was written in the books, according to what they had done.

—REVELATION 20:11–13

And he said with a loud voice, "Fear God and give him glory, because the hour of his judgment has come, and worship him who made heaven and earth, the sea and the springs of water."

—REVELATION 14:7

"But when the Son of Man comes in His glory, and all the angels with Him, then He will sit on His glorious throne. All the nations will be gathered before Him, and He will separate them from one another, as the shepherd separates the sheep from the goats; and He will put the sheep on His right, and the goats on the left. Then the King will say to those on His right, 'Come, you who are blessed of My Father, inherit the kingdom prepared for you from the foundation of the world. For I was hungry, and you gave Me something to eat; I was thirsty, and you gave Me something to drink; I was a stranger, and you invited Me in; naked, and you clothed Me; I was sick, and you visited Me; I was in prison, and you came to Me.' Then the righteous will answer Him, 'Lord, when did we see You hungry, and feed You, or thirsty, and give You something to drink? And when did we see You a stranger, and invite you in, or naked, and clothe You? When did we see You sick, or in prison, and come to You?' The King will answer and say to them, 'Truly I say to you, to the extent that you did it to one of these brothers of Mine, even the least of them, you did it to Me.'

"Then He will also say to those on His left, 'Depart from Me, accursed ones, into the eternal fire which has been prepared for the devil and his angels; for I was hungry, and you gave Me nothing to eat; I was thirsty, and you gave Me nothing to drink; I was a stranger, and you did not invite Me in; naked, and you did not clothe Me; sick, and in prison, and you did not visit Me.' Then they themselves also will answer, 'Lord, when did we see You hungry, or thirsty, or a stranger, or naked, or sick, or in prison, and did not take care of You?' Then He will answer them, 'Truly I say to you, to the extent that you did not do it to one of the least of these, you did not do it to Me.' These will go away into eternal punishment, but the righteous into eternal life." (Matt. 25:31–46 NASB95)

Near the end of Matthew's gospel, Jesus told his disciples about the coming final judgment. Jesus knew that events were accelerating him toward his trial, persecution, and crucifixion, and his time with the disciples was drawing to a close. As he described this day of judgment to his disciples, he did so by identifying himself as the Son of Man who would come in glory with his angels and sit on his glorious throne. Thus, this passage brings together the revelation of Christ as King with the accomplishment of his saving purpose. The coming of the Son of Man in glory is promised and he will indeed reign on a glorious throne. The context of this passage is important: Christ was at that moment headed for the cross, but he had in mind his reign and kingdom and the judgment that would surely come.

Jesus presented to his disciples a picture of all the nations gathered before the throne for judgment. Jesus, speaking of himself as the reigning and glorious king, said, "He will separate people from one another as a shepherd separates the sheep from the goats."

This image is easy enough for us to understand. Sheep and goats may pasture alongside one another, but they are very different animals. In the Bible, there is often a contrast between sheep and goats in which sheep refer to those who belong to God by faith, and goats are those who resist the kingdom and God's rule.

This seems to fit the personality of these two animals. Sheep are marked by the fact that, though prone to wander, they are meek and gentle. Goats, on the other hand, have a much more intemperate nature. If you wander into the wrong field, you may find a sheep who will accidentally bump into you. On the other hand, you might encounter a goat who will come at you with both force and intention.

Christ described the coming judgment as a shepherd making a distinction between sheep and goats. The sheep are placed on his right hand, the place of honor, and the goats are placed on the left. After the separation, "Then the King will say to those on his right, 'Come, you who are blessed by my Father, inherit the kingdom prepared for you from the foundation of the world.'"

Later we are told that he will say to those on his left, the goats, "Depart from me, you cursed, into the eternal fire prepared for the devil and his angels."

We cannot imagine any starker words of judgment, and these words come to us with a thunderous finality. Those who are on the King's right will enter into his joy, while those on his left are destined for eternal punishment.

## The Authority of the King

We often think of monarchs as fulfilling what is primarily a political duty, as head of state and sometimes as head of government. But in the ancient world, kings fulfilled a much more comprehensive function. They were understood to embody the people and were often called upon to make judgments among them. In such a monarchial system, the royal judgment was the final judgment.

In this parable, Jesus revealed himself to be the King whose rule will be not only comprehensive but also all-encompassing and eternal. An earthly king may make a judgment that will be final on earth, but King Jesus will make judgments that are binding for eternity.

The throne in this passage represents the kingly authority that Christ will exercise on this day of judgment. His throne is not merely a piece of furniture, but a representation of his glory and authority. He will make his declarations from a throne that is glorious beyond our imagination. The throne described by Jesus, the throne from which he will reign forever, is a throne that represents not only a nation but the entire cosmos.

# The Separation of the Sheep and the Goats

The nature of God's final judgment is made clear in the shepherd's act of separating the sheep and the goats. When the Son of Man comes, he will judge and rule the nations with a rod of iron. That judgment is made clear in the book of Revelation, which tells us of Christ's return on a white horse: "From his mouth comes a sharp sword with which to strike down the nations, and he will rule them with a rod of iron. He will tread the winepress of the fury of the wrath of God the Almighty. On his robe and on his thigh he has a name written, King of kings and Lord of lords" (19:15–16).

We have seen Jesus make repeated distinctions between the sons of light and the sons of darkness, the children of this age and those who are to be the children of the kingdom of heaven. Throughout the New Testament, we encounter the pattern of a judgment that will lead to dual destinies. The distinction between sheep and goats is a sign of the distinction that will be on the Day of Judgment irrevocable and eternal.

The book of Revelation describes the scene: "Then I saw a great white throne and him who was seated on it. From his presence earth and sky fled away, and no place was found for them. And I saw the dead, great and small, standing before the throne, and books were opened. Then another book was opened, which is the book of life. And the dead were judged by what was written in the books, according to what they had done. And the sea gave up the dead who were in it, Death and Hades gave up the dead who were in them, and they were judged, each one of them, according to what they had done" (20:11–13).

But then we are told that the dual destiny is final: "Then Death and Hades were thrown into the lake of fire. This is the second death, the lake of fire. And if anyone's name was not found written in the book of life, he was thrown into the lake of fire" (vv. 14–15).

We saw a similar theme made clear in Luke 16 in the parable of the rich man and Lazarus. A final, irrevocable judgment and a dual destiny. Lazarus comforted in Abraham's bosom, the rich man suffering torment in hell. Over and over again, Jesus will speak of those who go into everlasting life versus those who are destined by judgment for eternal punishment.

We face enormous resistance to this consistent, undeniable biblical theme of one judgment with two destinies. We face an outright theological rebellion in some quarters against the fact that the Scripture is so clear in God's revelation of this impending judgment. As we have seen, the human ideal of fairness is woefully inadequate to account for the horrible reality of human sin and the righteousness of God's own character. Theological compromise in our era has included those who have tried to deny any divine judgment such as described here in this text. Liberal theologies have attempted to present a God who would never make such a severe judgment and who would certainly not reduce the possible judgments to two. Some argue that those who have not come to Christ in this life must have some opportunity to confess Christ and be saved in the life to come. We must note the Scripture holds out no possibility of any postmortem conversion.

H. Richard Niebuhr described this liberal theology well: "A God without wrath brought men without sin into a kingdom without judgment through the ministrations of a Christ without a cross."[1]

Such a theology is incompatible and contradictory to all the Scriptures.

The reality of divine judgment in the terms Jesus described is certainly horrifying as we consider the eternal consequences. It is deeply humbling to any human pride, for those who belong to Christ understand that, in ourselves, there is no way we could avoid anything other than eternal damnation. We have all sinned and fallen short of the glory of God (Rom. 3:23). We are unable to rescue ourselves or to provide any remedy for our salvation. This drives us to the gospel and to cling to Christ, understanding that only Christ's righteousness will be recognized by the Father, and Christ's righteousness is imputed to believers by faith.

The judgment made so clear in this passage demonstrates the glory of God. Remember, in both the Matthew 25 and the Revelation 19 passages, Jesus is sitting on his glorious throne at the coming judgment. This is another sobering reality that Christians must always keep in mind. If something is God's perfect plan and purpose, it is infinitely glorious. No dimension of the gospel, absolutely no dimension of God's work, reflects anything less than that infinite glory. If we are embarrassed by the biblical teaching concerning judgment, we are embarrassed by the gospel, embarrassed by Christ, and embarrassed by the true and living God.

The church has not preached this doctrine of judgment out of triumphalism or a sense of superiority, for we know that we share with all humanity the fact that we deserve damnation and eternal separation from God.

Instead, the reality of impending judgment, in the stark and dramatic terms revealed by Jesus even in this passage, serves to impel us and energize us toward an even more faithful work of evangelism and missions. Our proclamation of the gospel and our witness to Christ are driven by the understanding that this judgment is coming. For ourselves, and for all others, we consider the question asked in the book of Hebrews: "How shall we escape if we neglect such a great salvation?" (2:3).

This coming judgment was made clear even in the Old Testament. In the first psalm we read, "Therefore the wicked will not stand in the judgment, nor sinners in the congregation of the righteous; for the LORD knows the way of the righteous, but the way of the wicked will perish" (vv. 5–6). Repeatedly, God described as executing judgment, "putting down one and lifting up another" (Ps. 75:7). In the book of Ecclesiastes, we are warned: "For God will bring every deed into judgment, with every secret thing, whether good or evil" (Eccl. 12:14).

Emphasizing the same theme, Jesus foretold the coming judgment when he warned, "I tell you, on the day of judgment people will give account for every careless word they speak" (Matt. 12:36).

In another memorable passage, Peter wrote about judgment with crystal clarity: "For they deliberately overlook this fact, that the heavens existed long ago, and the earth was formed out of water and through water by the word of God, and that by means of these the world that then existed was deluged with water and perished. But by the same word the heavens and earth that now exist are stored up for fire, being kept until the day of judgment and destruction of the ungodly" (2 Peter 3:5–7).

## The Works Reveal the Heart

In describing the judgment that is to come and the verdicts to be handed down from the glorious throne, Jesus described those who are the sheep, on his right, invited to inherit the kingdom prepared for them from the foundation of the world: "For I was hungry, and you gave Me something to eat; I was thirsty, and you gave Me something to drink; I was a stranger, and you invited Me in; naked, and you clothed Me; I was sick, and you visited Me; I was in prison, and you came to Me." These are all the works of the righteous, but the Bible makes clear that it is not works that make sinners righteous; it is rather works reveal the righteousness that has come by salvation through Jesus Christ. Even as the righteousness of Christ is the only righteousness that will suffice on the day of judgment, the righteousness demonstrated by the saints is the righteousness that was produced in them as visible evidence of the righteousness that has been imputed to them. Taking care of the hungry and the thirsty, welcoming strangers and clothing the naked—all those good works described in this passage are evidence of the new life, the new heart that produces these good works.

On the other hand, the goats who are destined for eternal punishment are told, "For I was hungry, and you gave Me nothing to eat; I was thirsty, and you gave Me nothing to drink; I was a stranger, and you did not invite Me in, naked, and you did not clothe Me; I was sick, and in prison, and you did not visit Me." There we see the mirror opposite of the declaration concerning the sheep. The goats demonstrate their rebellion against God by refusing to love those whom God loves. Their lack of good works is a demonstration of the unregenerate nature of their hearts.

When those on both the left and the right ask when they had either served Christ in this way or failed to do so, Jesus explained that the King will say: "Truly I say to you, to the extent that you did it to one of these brothers of Mine, even the least of them, you did it to Me." Conversely, those who are sent into everlasting punishment will be told, "Truly I say to you, to the extent that you did not do it to one of the least of these, you did not do it to Me." The key issue here is to recognize that Jesus spoke specifically of "one of these brothers of Mine, *even* the least *of them.*"

This indicates that there is a particular responsibility of Christians to other Christians. Brothers and sisters in Christ bear a particular responsibility to take care of those who are indeed our brothers and sisters. Even as Jesus had told the disciples about their responsibility, in the church, to forgive a brother or sister who sins against them, we see the "brothers" in this passage pointing to a parallel reality.

As we conclude our consideration of this parable, we need to understand that Christ was describing the wrath of God poured out upon sin. God's wrath is his perfect and righteous response to sin. His wrath is not merely his anger, though his anger is kindled. Wrath is his settled disposition toward sin and sinners; a disposition that, but for Christ, means eternal separation and the judgment described in such unmistakable terms as everlasting torment.

How may we escape the wrath of God, which is sure to come, poured out upon all unrighteousness? There is only one escape, and that is that we flee to refuge in Christ. In Christ we are safe, bearing his own righteousness. Alone we deserve nothing but hell.

On that day of judgment, the sheep and goats will be separated—the sheep to the right and the goats to the left. On that day, where will you be found standing?

# 17

# You Know Neither the Day nor the Hour

## THE PARABLE OF THE TEN VIRGINS

Now concerning the times and seasons, brothers, you have no need to have anything written to you. For you yourselves are fully aware that the day of the Lord will come like a thief in the night. While people are saying, "There is peace and security," then sudden destruction will come upon them as labor pains come upon a pregnant woman, and they will not escape. But you are not in darkness, brothers, for that day to surprise you like a thief.

—1 THESSALONIANS 5:1–4

He said to them, "It is not for you to know the times or seasons that the Father has fixed by his own authority."

—ACTS 1:7

"Then the kingdom of heaven will be comparable to ten virgins, who took their lamps and went out to meet the bridegroom. Five of them were foolish, and five were prudent. For when the foolish took their lamps, they took no oil with them, but the prudent took oil in flasks along with their lamps. Now while the bridegroom was delaying, they all got drowsy and began to sleep. But at midnight there was a shout, 'Behold, the bridegroom! Come out to meet him.' Then all those virgins rose and trimmed their lamps. The foolish said to the prudent, 'Give us some of your oil, for our lamps are going out.' But the prudent answered, 'No, there will not be enough for us and you too; go instead to the dealers and buy some for yourselves.' And while they were going away to make the purchase, the bridegroom came, and those who were ready went in with him to the wedding feast; and the door was shut. Later the other virgins also came, saying, 'Lord, lord, open up for us.' But he answered, 'Truly I say to you, I do not know you.' Be on the alert then, for you do not know the day nor the hour." (Matt. 25:1–13 NASB95)

*L*ike a thief in the night. With those memorable words we are reminded that the Lord is going to come suddenly and unexpectedly. The faithful church is to live in expectation and readiness, prepared for the Lord to return at any time. When the Lord returns, we are not to be found immobile, passively awaiting the Lord's coming. To the contrary, we are to be found faithful, obeying the commands of Christ until the moment he comes. But, when he comes, it will be like a thief in the night.

On his way to the cross, Jesus taught the disciples about his coming. Jesus told them, "But concerning that day and hour no one knows, not even the angels of heaven, nor the Son, but the Father only" (Matt. 24:36). These are sobering words, for they tell us that it is not given to us to know the day and hour of the Lord's return. The Father has not given this timetable to us, and thus the church is to live in constant and immediate expectation that the Lord may return at any time.

Jesus told the disciples that as the people in Noah's time experienced the flood coming upon them suddenly and unexpectedly, the same will be true when Christ returns. Thus, "the days of Noah" are a signal of the dangers for the unbelieving when Christ does come back to earth. Jesus spoke straightforwardly: "For as in those days before the flood they were eating and drinking, marrying and giving in marriage, until the day when Noah entered the ark, and they were unaware until the flood came and swept them all away, so will be the coming of the Son of Man" (vv. 38–39). Jesus went on to reveal indelible pictures that are constant in the Christian imagination. We are told of two men working in a field, "one will be taken and one left" (v. 40). Similarly, two women will be grinding at the mill, and again one will be taken and another one left. The warning from Jesus is that the church must stay awake and remain aware, "for you do not know on what day your Lord is coming" (v. 42).

After this, Jesus spoke of a thief, telling us that the master of a house would have stayed awake and prevented the break-in, had he only known when the thief was coming. Danger fell upon the house, precisely because the master did not know the timing of the thief's coming. "Therefore you also must be ready," Jesus warned, "for the Son of Man is coming at an hour you do not expect" (v. 44).

Immediately thereafter, Jesus shared about a wicked servant whose wicked behavior, including keeping company with drunkards, was exposed when the master, having been delayed in return, did return and found the servant engaged in his betrayal. The master, we are told, "will cut him in pieces and put him with the hypocrites. In that place there will be weeping and gnashing of teeth" (v. 51). Jesus used the picture of this extraordinarily harsh sentence of a misbehaving servant in order to get our attention and to make us understand what is at stake when it comes to the judgment he will bring when he returns.

Before turning to the parable of the ten virgins in Matthew 25, it is important for us to recognize that two central themes of the return of Christ have been made clear in these closing paragraphs of Matthew 24. Jesus has told us that his return will be sudden and surprising. He will come in judgment when he is not expected. The second theme that is revealed in the last sentences of chapter 24 is that the Lord's return will seem to the disciples to be delayed.

There can be no doubt that this has been one of the issues of greatest perplexity for Christians. Why does the Lord not return *now*? Why has the church been waiting so long? The clear answer from Scripture is that the perfect timetable of the Father has not yet been accomplished. History is not off course; we are simply unable to judge what is long and what is short over against the span of eternity. Jesus told the disciples that they must wait in readiness and in expectation, but he also made clear that the perception of a delay in his coming means only that the church must be evermore committed to obeying Christ's commands and being engaged in the tasks of the kingdom. Again, Jesus said that we should expect this delay, even as the master was delayed in returning to his home in 24:45–49.

The themes of Jesus' sudden return and the apparent delay of that return appear again in chapter 25 in the parable of the ten virgins. Jesus described the kingdom of heaven as being like "ten virgins, who took their lamps and went out to meet the bridegroom." Five were foolish and five were prudent (wise). The foolish virgins are described as having taken no oil with them for their lamps as they prepared to accompany the bride on the way to the wedding at the home of the bridegroom. The wise young women took extra oil with them, in preparation for what might be a delay in the procession.

Indeed, the bridegroom was delayed, and the ten young women became drowsy and slept. But, at the unexpected hour of midnight, there was a cry heard in the night: "Behold, the bridegroom! Come out to meet him." All the women rose and trimmed their lamps. But at that point the foolish women understood that they had not prepared themselves for the bridegroom's coming. They turned to the wise young women and asked them for some of their oil, "for our lamps are going out." But the wise virgins responded, "No, there will not be enough for us and you too; go instead to the dealers and buy some for yourselves." But, even as the five unwise young women went to buy the oil, the bridegroom came and the procession took place as he made his way to the marriage feast. The door was shut. When the five unwise women came and asked to be admitted to the feast, crying out, "Lord, lord, open up for us," the bridegroom answered, "'Truly I say to you, I do not know you.' Be on the alert then, for you do not know the day nor the hour."

We could wish that we knew more of the marriage customs of first-century Judaism. Scholars must be honest in admitting that we do not have much historical documentation about the details of the wedding, the wedding ceremony, or the wedding celebration. Betrothal was the period between the time the family of the young woman and the family of the young man agreed that a marriage would take place in the future. It was considered an unbreakable contract. Girls may have been betrothed between the ages of twelve and sixteen. Boys or young men were likely to be between sixteen and twenty years of age. There was little delay between the achievement of sexual maturity and the expectation of marriage.

Furthermore, marriage was taken with such seriousness that it was a matter for the entire community to understand and affirm. An elaborate ritual was in place, and we know enough from the biblical evidence to understand that once the time of the wedding had come, the stage was set for the bride to be taken to the bridegroom (or the bridegroom's home, or the home of the bridegroom's parents, if that is where the young couple would live). The procession of the bride from the house of the bride to the home of the bridegroom would require that she be accompanied by young virgins who would testify to the integrity of the wedding ceremony and the marriage. They're referred to here as virgins because they were expected to be just that, awaiting their own weddings in the future.

The two things we have considered—the fact that it is not given to us to know when the Lord will return, and the Lord's instruction that we should expect delay—come together in this parable: the bridegroom is delayed.

Given the context, we might well assume that the delay has been due to negotiations over the dowry. According to the marriage customs and contracts of the time, the greatest leverage in negotiating the dowry came at the last hours as the wedding had been prepared. In this case, the dowry negotiations may have been extended far longer than anyone had expected. The delay had gone into the night, and the ten young women who were to accompany the bride to the bridegroom found themselves in the dark in more ways than one. They were in the darkness of the night, and they were also in ignorance of when their services in the procession might be needed.

The ten virgins fell asleep as they were awaiting the processional and ceremony. But then came the midnight cry: "Behold, the bridegroom! Come out to meet him." At that point, the procession was ready to begin.

But, at that late and dark hour, the five young women who had not brought extra oil for their lamps realized that their lamps could not possibly burn through the procession. This was completely unacceptable, and they knew it. Thus, they turned to the other young women, the wise virgins who had brought oil, and asked to use some of their oil. But the wise virgins understood that they had brought enough oil for their own lamps and not enough for their foolish friends. The foolish young women were then told to go and buy the oil in the marketplace. They would be unlikely to achieve any success in the marketplace, precisely because of the lateness of the hour.

The point is that the bridegroom had been delayed, but he had now come. Now that he had come, the procession was going to start. There would be no waiting for the young women who were unprepared. The procession would continue with the five wise young women who had prepared themselves for the bridegroom's coming, at any hour, by securing the extra oil.

It is likely that the lamps referred to in this parable were at the end of poles, much like torches. These would have been used in order to serve both as illumination and celebration. Tipped with cloth that had been soaked in oil, the light of the torches would not last more than about a quarter hour without the addition of more oil. Thus, the unwise young women found themselves in a situation of humiliation and disaster. The procession did continue, all the way to the bridegroom's house where, once the wedding party was inside, the door was closed. The foolish young women, having finally attained their oil, came to the bridegroom's home and asked to be let in, but this was denied them.

When they cried out, "Lord, lord, open up for us," the response they received was not just the refusal of remittance, but a surprisingly harsh rejection: "I do not know you."

This chilling word of judgment is far more serious than many who heard this parable might have thought. Nevertheless, the disciples must certainly have thought back to what Jesus said in Matthew 7:21–23: "Not everyone who says to me, 'Lord, Lord,' will enter the kingdom of heaven, but the one who does the will of my Father who is in heaven. On that day, many will say to me, 'Lord, Lord, did we not prophesy in your name, and cast out demons in your name, and do many mighty works in your name?' And then will I declare to them, 'I never knew you; depart from me, you workers of lawlessness.'" We confront again the language of final judgment. Jesus warned that there will be those to whom he will say, "*I never knew you.*" No stronger verdict is imaginable. Speaking in judgment, Jesus was saying, "You are not mine, you were never mine, you will never be mine."

Jesus concluded the parable of the ten virgins with a lesson for the disciples, whom he does know: "Watch therefore, for you know neither the day nor the hour."

One of the central Christian affirmations is that Jesus is coming; indeed, he is our great and coming King. As surely as he came, born in Bethlehem, he will come in order to redeem his people, bring the fullness of his kingdom, and judge the nations with a rod of iron. His coming is the precious "blessed hope" of the Christian church. We live in the expectation and in the sure knowledge of the Lord's return, understanding that indeed we are experiencing a delay from the time of his ascension into heaven until the time when he will return in glory. But we experience that delay as an opportunity to work on behalf of the kingdom, to evangelize the nations by making disciples, and to be found obeying all that the Lord has commanded his church to do. Thus, the delay is for God's sovereign purpose, that the church be active in the world as the visible presence of the kingdom of Christ until such time that Christ returns in both judgment and glory.

Over and over again, the church is reminded to be ready at any time for the Lord to return. Paul, writing to the Thessalonian Christians, instructed them, "Now concerning the times and the seasons, brothers, you have no need to have anything written to you. For you yourselves are fully aware that the day of the Lord will come like a thief in the night" (1 Thess. 5:1–2). Once again, we encounter the image of a thief coming in the night. Jesus mentioned this in the sentences preceding the parable of the ten virgins in Matthew 25. Paul used the same metaphor in 1 Thessalonians 5:2. The thief coming in the night never announces his coming, for that would defeat his purpose. Instead, by stealth and surprise he carries out his purpose.

Like the proverbial thief in the night, Jesus will come, catching humanity by surprise.

Tellingly, Paul warned that the Lord will return at the very time that many people believe they are living in calm, peace, and serene security. "While people are saying, 'There is peace and security,' then sudden destruction will come upon them as labor pains come upon a pregnant woman, and they will not escape" (v. 3). The metaphor of the woman experiencing the pains of labor is also powerful. She knows that the labor pains will come, but almost every expectant mother can tell you that the precise coming of that labor is beyond her ability to predict. Young couples, especially those expecting their first child, know that what is often perceived to be labor is actually "false labor," but the skilled physician knows how to recognize the difference. There is one other dimension of the comparison of the Lord's coming to a woman experiencing the pains of labor. Once the labor process starts, it will continue on its own timetable. There is no possibility of renegotiating the timing once the labor begins.

The apostle Paul spoke directly to the Thessalonian Christians, reminding them that they were "not in darkness" (1 Thess. 5:4). The fact that we do not know when the Lord will return is itself a vital piece of knowledge among Christians. Faithful Christians are defined by the fact that we know that the Lord might return at any hour of any day, and we must be found ready. Paul encouraged his readers to understand that they have no fear of Christ coming as a thief in the night, for he is coming not to plunder the Christians, but rather to take them home.

Paul's words of encouragement to Christians continue in verses 4–6: "But you are not in darkness, brothers, for that day to surprise you like a thief. For you are all children of light, children of the day. We are not of the night or of the darkness. So then let us not sleep, as others do, but let us keep awake and be sober."

Throughout the history of the Christian church, there have been those who have sought to deny the biblical truth that Jesus will come on a day and at an hour that we do not know. Infamously, William Miller, preaching in New York in the nineteenth century, confidently predicted that the Lord Jesus Christ would return in 1843 or 1844. Eventually, he settled on the date October 22, 1844. On the basis of his confident prediction, many of his followers sold their property, put on white clothes, and waited for the Lord's return. An eschatological fervor had struck many at that time, and Miller became only the most famous of those to declare that he knew when the Lord would return. Clearly, the Lord Jesus Christ did not return on October 22, 1844, and this left Miller and the Millerites with a great deal to explain. They tried various arguments to recalibrate the date, but, now well over a century and a half later, we understand that the Millerites cost the Christian church a great deal of credibility in the United States. Instead of celebrating the return of the Lord Jesus Christ, the Millerites and their friends experienced what became known as the "Great Disappointment."

Judged by what we have learned in Scripture, the Millerites failed in more than one way. They should never have claimed to have been able to predict a date on which the Lord would return. Furthermore, they disobeyed the Lord's command by waiting for him to return as if they were helping to bring the current age to an end, when they should have been working on behalf of the gospel and the kingdom, if they truly understood the gospel and obeyed the Word.

Throughout human history, Christians have believed themselves to have sufficient information to predict when the Lord would return. Jesus told his disciples that there would be signs of his return, including wars and rumors of wars. But Jesus warned that such signs do not necessarily indicate the suddenness of his return. "All these are but the beginning of the birth pains," Jesus said (Matt. 24:8). Christians in the apostolic age understood the dramatic nature of their time to indicate that the Christian era may be short. Christians who experienced the horrifying persecution of Rome believed that they had adequate reason to believe the Lord might soon return. Predictions of the Lord's return have coincided with events such as the fall of Jerusalem to the Romans in AD 70 and then the fall of Rome itself at the end of the fourth and into the fifth century. Horrors such as plague, famine, earthquakes, and even signs in the sky have been interpreted as sure signs of the Lord's imminent return.

But Christians are never to forget that the Lord told us in advance that he is coming soon, but on the timetable of the Father's choosing. He told us that we will not know the day or the hour, but we need not fear if we are found faithful. Unlike the foolish young women in the parable of the ten virgins, we are to be constantly prepared, conscious of the fact that the Lord may return at any time, and ready to join in the adulation and celebration of the Lord as the returning King. We are not to be found unprepared, inactive, and unfaithful. The Christian church is to live every moment until Jesus comes in the sure and certain hope of his return, the "blessed hope" that has sustained the saints of God throughout the centuries.

In the age of the church, Christians are to be found going out into the fields of the Lord even as workers are needed for the harvest. We are to preach the gospel and make disciples of all the nations. We are to marry and to give in marriage and to raise our children in the nurture and admonition of the Lord. We are to pass down the Christian faith from generation to generation, knowing that a part of our task is to prepare every successive generation of Christians for the return of Christ. We are to seize every opportunity for the kingdom and be found faithful in every opportunity the Lord has given us.

Armed with this hope, the Christian church can face persecution, adversity, plague, famine, and even death. This is the great hope that is expressed in the confidence the Lord gave his church when he declared, "On this rock I will build my church, and the gates of hell shall not prevail against it" (Matt. 16:18).

In the revelation given to the apostle John, Jesus said: "Behold, I am coming soon, bringing my recompense with me, to repay each one for what he has done. I am the Alpha and the Omega, the first and the last, the beginning and the end" (Rev. 22:12–13).

This is the great promise. This is our great hope. This is the faith of the Christian church. And this faith takes the form of a prayer that comes down to one precious word, *maranatha*. As John related to us from his vision, "He who testifies to these things says, 'Surely I am coming soon.'" And we are taught to respond to that promise with these words: "Amen. Come, Lord Jesus!" (v. 20). Indeed, amen. Come, Lord Jesus!

# Acknowledgments

No book writes itself and no author writes alone. Behind this book is a debt owed to many people whose lives and influence and devotion have been channeled into my life. Some were preachers and teachers, including pastors, authors, and seminary professors long dead. Some I never even met. One of those was Ray Stedman, longtime pastor of Peninsula Bible Church in Palo Alto, California. As a teenager in Florida, I knew nothing about the man or his ministry, but an older Christian passed along cassette tapes of some of Ray Stedman's sermons on the parables of Jesus. I listened to them again and again. He was the first preacher who showed me the explosive nature of Jesus' parables.

Three New Testament professors from my seminary days deserve special mention. I had the opportunity to study the Gospel of Luke under the late Professor Eduard Schweizer of the University of Zurich. His appreciation for the literary structure of the parables in Luke opened my eyes to a whole new dimension of understanding. The late Professor George R. Beasley-Murray, former principal of Spurgeon's College in London, helped me to understand the parables, especially as found in Matthew. Professor Peter Rhea Jones taught a full course on the parables of Jesus, combining his experience as both scholar and preacher. He combined kindness and serious scholarship and helped me to see the role of the parables within the teaching of Jesus. He was the first to raise, in my mind, the question of what the disciples of Jesus were to think about the parables. Dr. Jones and I ended up on opposite sides in the great controversy within the Southern Baptist Convention, but a student never outgrows a debt of gratitude to his teacher.

At Southern Seminary and Boyce College, I am surrounded by the most amazing and faithful teachers and scholars as colleagues, and by the most demanding and exhilarating students. Now in my thirtieth year as president, I remain unspeakably thankful for the privilege of teaching and learning among such wonderful people.

In my office, I am also surrounded by incredible colleagues. Graham Faulkner serves as Director of Communications and as producer of both *The Briefing* and *Thinking in Public*. Ryan Modisette serves as technical engineer. Their work and encouragement are deeply appreciated. Caleb Shaw serves as chief of staff and executive assistant. Without his patient and skilled leadership, the trains would never show up on time. Thanks to him, they do. Anna Arrastia serves as executive administrative assistant, incredibly helpful and always a step ahead. Cory Higdon, soon to be Cory Higdon, Ph.D., has served with great devotion and skill as Director of Presidential Research. He is an outstanding young scholar, who has been consistently helpful and encouraging in all my writing projects.

I am also assisted by a team of student interns, who are as clear a sign of God's promise in the coming generation of seminary students as I can imagine. I am very thankful for William Wolfe, Sam Bankston, Carlo Cicero, Ben Pinkston, Jono Burlini, Austin Maddox, Steven Condy, and Alex Richey.

I am thankful for the Board of Trustees of the Southern Baptist Theological Seminary, and for their encouragement in this project and in so many others. I am so thankful for churches who, throughout the past four decades and more, have graciously heard my preaching, including my preaching on the parables.

Finally, I am thankful beyond words for my family, starting with my wife, Mary. Our daughter Katie and her husband Riley have blessed us beyond measure and have brought the three most wonderful grandchildren into our lives. Benjamin, Henry, and Margaret are sheer delight. Our son Christopher mixes encouragement with humor, and both gifts are appreciated.

As always, my earthly acknowledgments must end with thanking Mary, without whom my life would make no sense and with whom life is such a joy. Her encouragement and wisdom are channeled into everything I do. No words suffice.

# Notes

## INTRODUCTION

1. Peter Rhea Jones, *The Teaching of the Parables* (Nashville: Broadman Press, 1982), 34.
2. William Barclay, *The Gospel of Matthew*, 2 vols. (Edinburgh: St. Andrew Press, 1958), Volume One, 63.
3. John MacArthur, *Parables: The Mysteries of God's Kingdom Revealed Through the Stories Jesus Told* (Nashville: Nelson Books, 2015), xiii.

## CHAPTER 2: HEARTS READY TO RECEIVE THE WORD

1. *Westminster Confession of Faith*, Section 17, paragraph 1.

## CHAPTER 3: THE CHILDREN OF LIGHT AND THE CHILDREN OF DARKNESS

1. R. T. France, *Matthew: Tyndale New Testament Commentaries* (Downers Grove: InterVarsity Press, 1985), 299.
2. James Orr, *Christian View of God and the World* (New York: Charles Scribner's Sons, 1908), 9.

## CHAPTER 5: EVEN IF ONE SHOULD RISE FROM THE DEAD

1. Dale Vree, "Hell, Air-Conditioned," *New Oxford Review* 58 (June 1996), 4.

## CHAPTER 6: REDEMPTION, REJOICING, AND REJECTION IN LUKE 15

1. Helmut Thielicke, *The Waiting Father*, translated by John W. Doberstein (San Franscisco: Harper & Row, 1959).
2. Kenneth E. Bailey, *Poet and Peasant and Through Peasant Eyes: A*

*Literary-Cultural Approach to the Parables in Luke, Combined Edition* (Grand Rapids: Eerdmans, 1976/1980, 1994).

## CHAPTER 13: WELL DONE, GOOD AND FAITHFUL SERVANT

1. A. J. Broomhall, *Hudson Taylor and China's Open Century, Book Two: Over the Treaty Wall* (London: Hodder and Stoughton and Overseas Missionary Fellowship, 1982), 6.
2. John Wesley, *The Journal of the Reverend John Wesley*, vol. 1, ed. John Emory (New York: T. Mason and G Lane, 1837), 138.

## CHAPTER 15: THE KINGDOM OF HEAVEN IS LIKE THIS

1. Augustine, *Teaching Christianity, Book 1:27, 28*, ed. John E. Rotelle, trans. Edmund Hill (Hyde Park: New York, New City Press, 1996), 118.
2. Louis Berkhof, *Systematic Theology* (Louisville: GLH Publishing, 2017), 342.

## CHAPTER 16: WHEN THE SON OF MAN COMES IN HIS GLORY

1. H. Richard Niebuhr, *Kingdom of God in America* (Chicago: Willett, Clark & Company, 1937), 193.

# About the Author

R. Albert Mohler Jr. has been called "one of America's most influential evangelicals" (*Economist*) and the "reigning intellectual of the evangelical movement" (Time.com). The president of the Southern Baptist Theological Seminary, he writes a popular blog and a regular commentary, available at AlbertMohler.com, and hosts two podcasts: *The Briefing* and *Thinking in Public*. He is the author of many books, including *The Gathering Storm: Secularism, Culture, and the Church*; *The Apostles Creed: Discovering Authentic Christianity in an Age of Counterfeits*; *We Cannot Be Silent*; and *The Prayer That Turns the World Upside Down*. He and his wife, Mary, live in Louisville, Kentucky.